Building Bridges
The How and Why of a Holistic Approach Towards Building Positive
Student/Teacher Relationships

Brandon Carpenter

Printed by Shalom Falls, in the United States of America.

First printing, 2026.

ISBN: 979-8-9995071-6-7 (Paperback)
ISBN: 979-8-9995071-7-4 (Digital Print)
ISBN: 979-8-9995071-8-1(Hardcover)

Introduction

In addition to being an educator, I am also a community leader (pastor) of a Messianic congregation in Wichita Falls, Texas. This bi-vocational career offers me a unique perspective on both teaching and leadership, allowing me to integrate my passion for education with my calling in ministry. The intersection of these roles creates an opportunity to cultivate a classroom environment that emphasizes values such as respect, compassion, and responsibility, which are foundational in both my teaching and pastoral work. This dual role allows me to inspire students in more profound ways, not only intellectually but also spiritually and emotionally.

As a teacher, I have unequivocally adopted the attitude that connecting with students and forging positive, healthy student-teacher relationships is the most effective way to facilitate student growth. I believe that when students feel safe, valued, and supported, they are more likely to engage with the material and perform at their best. Establishing trust and mutual respect creates a foundation for learning where students are encouraged to take risks, ask questions, and express themselves freely. Even in the most challenging classrooms, fostering strong relationships can have a transformative effect. Research consistently shows that students thrive academically when they feel emotionally supported, and this belief is central to my approach. (Gueldner, Feuerborn, & Merrell, 2010) I am convinced that any teacher, regardless of subject or grade level, can see positive academic growth and a rise in test scores if they prioritize relationship-building in their classroom. When students know their teacher cares deeply about their success and well-being, they are more motivated to rise to the challenge and excel.

This book presents a holistic approach (see chart below) that I have developed and refined over the past 20 years to build positive, meaningful relationships with my students. Throughout my career, I have adapted and evolved, recognizing that the methods that worked at Frenship Junior High in 1998 may not be as effective at Jacksboro Middle School in 2024. Each generation of students brings unique challenges, perspectives, and opportunities, requiring educators to remain flexible and responsive to their needs. While the specific

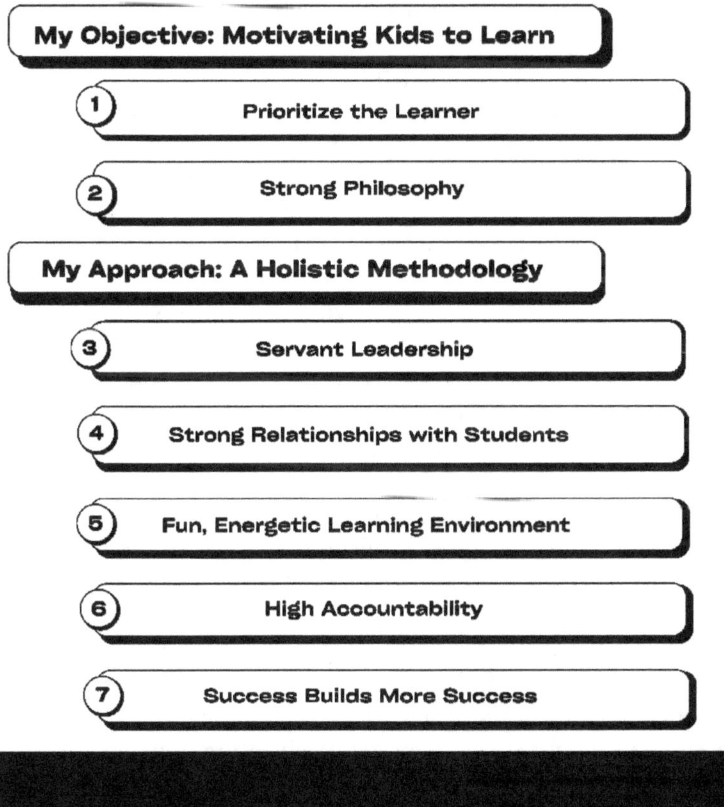

techniques I employ have changed to keep pace with shifting educational trends, student dynamics, and cultural influences, the core philosophy of my approach has remained steadfast.

At the heart of this holistic approach is the belief that education is not just about imparting knowledge—it's about nurturing the whole student. This means addressing their academic, emotional, and social needs in a way that fosters trust, mutual respect, and a sense of belonging. In 1998, this may have meant incorporating one-on-one conversations or using traditional teaching strategies to engage students. Today, it might involve leveraging technology, fostering collaborative learning environments, or using culturally responsive teaching methods.

One constant, however, is the emphasis on relationships as the foundation of effective teaching. Regardless of the tools or techniques, students flourish when they feel understood and valued. Building positive relationships allows me to connect with students on a deeper level, inspiring them to reach their full potential. Over the years, I've learned that while lesson plans and curricula are important, it is the human connection that truly makes a difference in the classroom. This book offers practical strategies, insights, and reflections from my own journey as an educator to help others embrace a holistic, relationship-centered approach to teaching that remains relevant and impactful, no matter the context or era.

The holistic approach begins with the understanding that motivating kids to learn and prioritizing their growth are my foremost responsibilities as an educator. Every decision I make in the classroom stems from this foundational belief. To be truly effective, I must adopt a well-defined philosophy of education—one that serves as a compass to guide my daily instructional decisions and planning. A philosophy-driven approach allows me to align my teaching methods with my core values, creating a consistent and purposeful learning environment.

Central to my philosophy is the vision of being a servant leader in the classroom. This means placing the needs of my students first, fostering an environment of trust, respect, and support. Building strong relationships with my students is not optional—it is essential. These connections form the foundation for meaningful learning and inspire students to invest in their own education. My vision also emphasizes the importance of creating a fun, energetic classroom where students feel motivated and excited to engage. To encourage participation and positive behavior, I use tools like "Carpenter Cash" (described later in the book) in a classroom economic system to reward effort and create a joyful atmosphere where students look forward to attending class each day.

Accountability is another pillar of this approach. My vision demands personal accountability, not only from my students but from myself as well. I hold myself to the same high standards I expect of my students, modeling perseverance, responsibility, and integrity. Lastly, my vision reminds me of the power of small victories. Little successes—whether mastering a new concept or overcoming a minor challenge—lay the groundwork for bigger achievements throughout the school year. This step-by-step progress builds confidence and fosters a growth mindset, ensuring that both my students and I continually move forward in our educational journey.

When I first started teaching, I was twenty-one years old, full of confidence but burdened by a cynical attitude toward students. I adopted an authoritarian, heavy-handed approach, determined to assert my control in the classroom. I mocked the often-repeated phrase, "Kids don't care how much you know until they know how much you care," dismissing it as sentimental nonsense. In those early years, my sole focus was to establish dominance, and I wanted everyone—students and parents alike—to understand that I was in charge. My belief was that every student would learn whether they wanted to or not. Unfortunately, this approach manifested in harsh, disrespectful interactions with both students and their families. The result was a hostile classroom environment where students had little desire to work for me or learn from me.

Two life-changing events forced me to reevaluate my methods and philosophy. First, I served as a principal in several school districts, which gave me the unique opportunity to observe the very best and the very worst teaching practices. These observations offered me a fresh perspective on what effective teaching truly looked like. I began to adopt the techniques that fostered engagement and trust while discarding the authoritarian behaviors that hindered learning.

Second, I became a father to two children, which profoundly altered my empathy and understanding. Seeing how a single teacher could either positively or negatively impact my children's school experience gave me a new sense of purpose. I realized that as an educator, I had the power to either uplift or discourage my students.

From that point forward, I became resolute in my commitment to being a teacher who inspires, encourages, and positively influences every student. My goal shifted to not only teaching academic content but also creating a classroom environment where students felt valued, supported, and motivated to achieve their best.

For several years, I stepped away from public education to focus on full-time ministry. When I returned to teaching, I quickly realized that I needed to refine and adapt my holistic approach to meet the needs of a new generation of students. My core methodology remained the same: prioritizing solid classroom instruction built on positive student-teacher relationships. My new teaching assignment brought me to a self-contained sixth-grade classroom in the small, rural Midway Independent School District, located outside of Henrietta, Texas. It was a setting unlike any I had experienced before. Although I had only taught math previously, I was now tasked with teaching all core subjects. Despite the challenge, I embraced the opportunity with determination and a commitment to give my best.

The class size was small—only eleven students—but my ambition and determination were anything but. Over the next two years, I implemented the holistic approach I present in this book, focusing on building strong relationships, fostering a love for learning, and motivating students to succeed. The results were incredible. Not only did my students achieve academic success, but they also became more confident, engaged, and excited to learn.

Encouraged by this success, I transitioned to teaching fifth-grade math, middle school math, and high school algebra courses at Midway. I continued to use my holistic approach, and it proved effective across all age groups. Test scores improved, classroom morale soared, and students consistently expressed enthusiasm about coming to class each day.

The ultimate validation of my efforts came in the form of a Facebook post from a parent after I resigned from Midway to accept a position at another district. In the post, they shared how much of a positive impact I had made on their child, highlighting the effectiveness of this approach in transforming both academic outcomes and student attitudes toward learning.

> Brant went into public school in the 5th grade and HATED
> it. Every dang Sunday evening, he'd come to my room and
> just stand there and not say a word. I would ask him what

was wrong, and he'd beg me not to make him go to school. That 5th grade year was tough on him, but probably tougher on me. I cried many tears feeling like a failure as a mother. But something magical happened in the 6th grade. Brantley was blessed to have Mr. Brandon Carpenter as a teacher. This guy changed school and learning for Brantley. The first thing that did it was Carpenter cash, an incentive to do well and be awarded with "cash" that they could then spend on awards/food/sonic drinks/etc. If you know Brantley, you know he is all about having a wallet full of cash and finding ways to earn more. There probably wasn't a better way to motivate Brantley than with Carpenter cash. He'd come home excited telling me about what he had "bought" at school, and I saw a drastic change in my child in terms of wanting to learn. Mr. C pushed Brantley, and he bloomed and grew exponentially. Brant is a math kid. He's good at it and it comes natural to him. However, he is not a fan of reading but read 24 books in the 6th grade. That was huge! Mr. C even gave Brantley the reading award that year, not because he was the best reader but because he had the most growth. In the 7th and 8th grade, Mr. C taught their class math, and I don't think there was a week that went by that Brantley wasn't telling me about something Mr. C had taught them or something he had said. Mr. C connected with my child and made learning fun. But, if you ask anyone whose child had Mr. C as a teacher, they'd say the same. This guy is truly a gem. And I owe him a lot because of how he was able to help Brantley in that transition and create a love of learning. I'm so thankful for what he did for Brant, and I know that Brantley is the student he is today because of Mr. C! We will miss Mr. Carpenter terribly next year but wish him the best on his new journey! (Facebook Post, May 18, 2023, accessed 12/27/2024)

Educators, I firmly believe that by adopting the holistic approach outlined in this book, tailoring it to align with your unique strengths and talents, and committing to its consistent implementation, you can achieve transformative success in your classroom. This approach is not a rigid formula, but a flexible framework designed to adapt to the diverse needs of teachers and students. It emphasizes building meaningful relationships, fostering a positive learning environment, and inspiring students to take ownership of their education.

When educators embrace this philosophy, they create classrooms where students feel valued, motivated, and equipped to succeed academically and personally. By making this approach your own and integrating it into your daily practices, you can foster a sense of connection and enthusiasm that resonates with students long after they leave your class. Success isn't measured solely by test scores or grades—it's reflected in the growth, confidence, and joy your students experience as they learn.

Let this book serve as both a guide and an inspiration, encouraging you to refine your teaching methods and embrace the potential within every student. Together, we can make a profound and lasting impact on the lives of those we teach.

Reflection

What is one specific way I can show my students that I care about their success and well-being this week?

How can I create a classroom environment where students feel safe to ask questions and express themselves?

What is one new relationship-building strategy I can try with my current students?

How will I adjust my approach to connect with students who seem less engaged or more reserved?

How can I use my own values—such as respect, compassion, and responsibility—to set a positive example in my classroom?

Chapter 1 - My Objective: Motivating Kids to Learn

In the ever-evolving landscape of education, effective teaching transcends the mere dissemination of information—it requires inspiring and motivating students to actively engage with the material. This understanding emphasizes the importance of encouraging students to overcome challenges and embrace the process of learning as an integral part of their personal development. Motivating students, much like coaching in sports, involves leading them to do what they might not naturally want to do to achieve what they aspire to accomplish. This concept resonates deeply with Tom Landry's famous quote: "The job of a football coach is getting men to do what they don't want to do, in order to achieve what they want to achieve." (Whitney, 2014) This chapter explores how educators act as coaches, using motivation as a critical tool in fostering a resilient and productive learning environment for their students.

The Essence of Motivating Learners

As a middle school math teacher, I have encountered countless students who initially lack enthusiasm for learning mathematics. Some have faced repeated failures in previous math courses, leaving them feeling defeated and incapable. Others struggle with the abstract nature of combining numbers and letters, finding it intimidating and confusing. Still, many have internalized damaging messages like, "You're just not a math person," which undermines their confidence and motivation before they even begin.

Allen Mendler provides additional psychological insights into this resistance. He explains, "From a psychological perspective, many [unmotivated] students . . . are covering their concerns about being perceived as stupid. They are protecting themselves from the embarrassment of looking dumb in the eyes of their classmates, parents, and selves. Some students find power and control in their refusals to work. They are often competent and capable, but their need to be in control is so strong that they employ a self-defeating strategy to exert their independence." (Mendler, 2011)

These insights remind us that a lack of enthusiasm for math (or any academic subject) often stems from deeper emotional and psychological barriers such as fear, insecurity, or a sense of powerlessness. Many students view math as a daunting challenge, fearing failure or ridicule if they make mistakes. This fear can lead to avoidance and disengagement, which only exacerbates the problem. For others, past experiences of failure or negative reinforcement may have chipped away at their confidence, making them believe that success in math is unattainable.

Recognizing these underlying issues is crucial for educators who wish to reignite a passion for learning in their students. Approaching reluctant learners with empathy, patience, and understanding helps create a classroom environment where students feel safe to take risks and make mistakes. By celebrating effort and progress rather than just results, teachers can rebuild students' confidence and remind them that learning is a journey.

In addition to empathy, effective strategies include presenting math in relatable, real-world contexts that resonate with students' interests and experiences. Offering opportunities for hands-on, inquiry-based activities can spark curiosity and show students how math applies to their lives. Encouragement, coupled with targeted support and a belief in their potential, helps students shift their perspective from seeing math as a barrier to viewing it as a tool for personal growth and empowerment. By fostering this transformation, teachers can empower students to embrace math with newfound confidence and enthusiasm.

Whatever the reason, many students enter my classroom every August with little motivation to learn math. It takes the job of a coach to motivate these kids to move past the fear of failure to an enjoyment of studying math and algebra.

Motivation is a cornerstone of effective education, serving as the engine that drives students' willingness to engage with new concepts and persevere through difficulties. It transforms the learning experience from a passive absorption of facts into a dynamic and interactive journey. Motivating students involves creating an environment where they feel empowered to take ownership of their learning, explore their interests, and cultivate a genuine enthusiasm for acquiring knowledge.

My role as an educator in this process is akin to that of a coach. Just as a sports coach inspires athletes to push beyond their limits and achieve personal bests, a teacher's responsibility is to motivate students to surpass their self-imposed boundaries: fear of failure, need to be in control, and boredom to a realized perspective of their potential. As a math teacher, much of my time is spent helping students to change their mindset about learning. I am a big fan of Jo Boaler's Mathematical Mindset research and I agree with her statement, "I have found that when students start to believe they can achieve, and they understand that I believe in them, bad behavior and lack of motivation disappear." (Boaler, 2015) Overall, this demands a delicate balance between nurturing and challenging students—supporting them through their struggles while encouraging them to tackle more difficult tasks and think critically about complex issues.

Applying Coaching Principles in Education

The analogy between coaching and teaching is profound and extends beyond simple motivation to include strategies that foster growth, perseverance, and success. Both roles involve guiding individuals toward reaching their full potential, often requiring careful planning, patience, and a deep understanding of each person's unique needs and challenges. Coaches and teachers alike must inspire and empower those they work with, helping them to develop the skills, mindset, and resilience needed to navigate setbacks and continue progressing toward their objectives. Tom Landry's quote encapsulates the essence of this relationship, highlighting that while students might resist certain activities in the short term, they ultimately seek to overcome challenges to achieve longer-term goals. This resistance often stems from the difficulty of the tasks at hand or the discomfort of leaving their comfort zones. However, a good teacher or coach knows how to frame these challenges as opportunities for growth, breaking them down into manageable steps and celebrating small victories along the way. By creating an environment of trust and encouragement, they can help students and athletes alike to persevere, even when the road ahead seems daunting. In the end, the lessons learned in these moments of struggle often become the foundation for future success, confidence, and self-reliance.

Coaches employ a variety of strategies to inspire their athletes; similarly, educators can use these tactics to motivate their students in the following ways:

Setting Clear Goals: Just as athletes train with specific objectives in mind, students benefit from clear, achievable goals that guide their learning journey. Goals serve as a roadmap, providing direction and purpose, while helping students measure progress along the way. Teachers play a vital role in helping students identify, articulate, and set these goals, ensuring they are both realistic and challenging. At the start of the school year, I send out a parent survey to better understand each student's personal goals for math. One of my key questions is designed to gauge their child's aspirations in the subject. This helps create a partnership between teachers and parents to support the student's journey. Short-term goals, like mastering a particular skill or completing a specific project, allow students to experience small, incremental successes that build confidence and reinforce their commitment to learning. Meanwhile, long-term aspirations—such as preparing for college, pursuing a dream career, or developing critical life skills—give students a broader vision of what they can achieve through sustained effort and discipline.

To make goals meaningful, teachers can encourage students to reflect on their interests, strengths, and passions, aligning their objectives with personal motivations. A goal that resonates with a student's personal interests is more likely to inspire persistence and enthusiasm. Additionally, teachers can help students break down larger goals into manageable steps, creating a clear plan of action that reduces overwhelm and builds momentum. For example, a student aiming to improve their overall math grade could set small, measurable goals, such as improving their homework completion rate or mastering specific problem types each week. By frequently revisiting and refining these goals, teachers help ensure that students remain engaged and adaptable, especially when faced with obstacles. Ultimately, clear goals not only keep students focused and motivated but also foster a sense of ownership over their learning. This sense of control empowers students to take charge of their educational journeys, building the skills and self-confidence necessary to succeed in the classroom and beyond.

Developing Resilience: Coaches train athletes to develop resilience in the face of adversity, emphasizing the importance of persistence despite setbacks. Similarly, in education, resilience is a crucial skill that empowers students to navigate the inevitable challenges of learning and life. Teachers play a vital role in fostering this trait by creating a supportive environment where setbacks are not seen as failures but as essential steps toward growth. When students encounter difficulties, teachers can guide them in reflecting on what went wrong, identifying alternative strategies, and finding ways to improve. This approach helps students understand that mistakes are not the end of the journey but valuable learning opportunities.

Promoting a growth mindset is essential in building resilience. Educators encourage students to embrace challenges with curiosity and determination, helping them shift their focus from immediate success to long-term growth. This mindset teaches them to prioritize effort and progress rather than just outcomes, making it easier for them to tackle complex tasks and subjects. Teachers can also model resilience by sharing their own experiences of overcoming difficulties, showing students that setbacks are a universal part of life. I often tell my algebra students every year that as a freshman in high school, I sat at my kitchen table crying while trying to do my algebra homework. It took perseverance to master algebra, and I assure them that I understand the struggle and am here to help. Celebrating small victories along the way reinforces the idea that resilience is not about instant success, but about continuous effort and improvement. Over time, students who develop resilience not only succeed academically but also gain confidence and adaptability, equipping them to thrive in the face of future challenges and opportunities. Resilience becomes a skill that extends far beyond the classroom, enabling students to face life's uncertainties with perseverance and determination.

Providing Constructive Feedback: Feedback is crucial in both sports and education to improve performance. In the realm of education, constructive feedback serves as a powerful tool to guide students toward growth and development. When delivered with empathy and precision, feedback not only addresses areas that need improvement but also reinforces a student's strengths, fostering confidence and motivation. Teachers who provide meaningful feedback help students develop a clearer sense of their progress, strengths, and potential for further growth. This feedback becomes a bridge between where students currently stand and where they aspire to be, illuminating the path forward.

Effective feedback goes beyond pointing out errors—it involves offering actionable suggestions for improvement, breaking down complex tasks into manageable components, and clarifying misunderstandings. For example, rather than simply stating that an essay lacks focus, a teacher might highlight specific instances where the main argument could be better supported with evidence, while also praising the clarity of the introduction. This balance helps students understand that growth is a continuous process rather than a final destination.

Constructive feedback also encourages self-awareness, teaching students to recognize their strengths and areas for improvement independently. This practice fosters a sense of ownership over their learning, motivating them to seek out ways to enhance their skills proactively. Moreover, feedback delivered in a supportive and respectful manner strengthens the teacher-student relationship, creating an environment of trust where students feel safe to take risks and embrace challenges. Ultimately, thoughtful feedback cultivates resilience, persistence, and a lifelong commitment to learning.

Cultivating an Intrinsic Love for Learning: Coaches work to instill a passion for the sport in their athletes, transcending the immediate desire for victory or success. Similarly, teachers aim to ignite a love for learning in their students, encouraging them to find joy and satisfaction in intellectual exploration that transcends grades or accolades. This intrinsic motivation is essential for fostering lifelong learners who are curious, self-directed, and eager to seek knowledge for its own sake. By helping students connect learning to their personal interests and passions, teachers can transform education from a task into a source of inspiration and fulfillment.

One way to cultivate this love for learning is by making lessons engaging, relevant, and meaningful. For example, teachers can design activities that relate to real-world problems or tie content to students' hobbies, cultures, or career aspirations. This approach not only makes learning more enjoyable but also helps students see the value and practical application of their education. Furthermore, creating a classroom environment that encourages exploration, questioning, and creativity allows students to take intellectual risks without fear of failure. When students feel free to experiment and express themselves, they are more likely to develop a genuine interest in the subject matter.

Another key strategy is to emphasize the process of learning rather than the outcome. Celebrating effort, curiosity, and improvement over test scores or grades helps students focus on the joy of discovery rather than external rewards. Teachers can model this mindset by sharing their own enthusiasm for learning, showing that intellectual growth is an ongoing, exciting journey. For instance, discussing how they overcame challenges or learned something new can inspire students to embrace a similar attitude.

Additionally, teachers can encourage students to pursue independent projects or delve deeper into topics they find intriguing. Allowing students to choose what they learn or how they approach a task fosters autonomy and ownership over their education, making it a more personal and rewarding experience. Whether it's conducting experiments, reading about historical events, or solving complex puzzles, these opportunities enable students to immerse themselves in subjects that resonate with their unique interests.

Finally, fostering a love for learning requires patience and persistence. Not every student will immediately feel passionate about every subject, but a teacher's consistent efforts to make learning meaningful and enjoyable can have a profound impact over time. By helping students find excitement in exploration and fulfillment in growth, teachers lay the foundation for a lifetime of curiosity, self-improvement, and intellectual engagement that extends far beyond the classroom walls.

Overcoming Resistance to Learning

Just as athletes may initially resist grueling practices, students sometimes shy away from academic challenges due to fear of failure, disinterest, or perceived difficulty. Teachers must navigate these barriers effectively, transforming resistance into engagement and growth. Motivation techniques tailored to individual student needs and interests can make a substantial difference in overcoming reluctance.

Differentiated Instruction: Recognizing that students have diverse learning styles, teachers can employ differentiated instruction tailored to individual preferences and strengths. Differentiation acknowledges that every student learns differently, whether through visual, auditory, kinesthetic, or reading/writing methods, and that a one-size-fits-all approach is insufficient in addressing the needs of a diverse classroom. By incorporating a variety of teaching methods—such as visual aids, hands-on activities, group discussions, and technology integration—educators can engage students more effectively, fostering a deeper connection with the material and reducing resistance to learning.

For example, visual learners may benefit from diagrams, videos, and charts, while kinesthetic learners may thrive in lessons that involve movement, experiments, or manipulatives. Similarly, auditory learners can excel when content is presented through lectures, discussions, or audio recordings, and reading/writing learners might prefer written instructions, reading assignments, or essay-based tasks. By providing these varied learning opportunities, teachers ensure that students can access content in a way that resonates with their individual preferences.

Differentiated instruction goes beyond simply varying teaching methods; it also involves adapting the pace and complexity of lessons to meet students' unique needs. For instance, advanced learners might be given extension tasks that challenge their critical thinking skills, while students who need more support may receive scaffolded activities that gradually build their confidence and understanding. Flexible grouping is another effective strategy, allowing students to collaborate in pairs or small teams based on shared abilities, interests, or learning goals. This approach encourages peer support and helps students learn from each other, fostering a collaborative and inclusive classroom environment.

Technology plays a significant role in supporting differentiated instruction, offering tools like interactive apps, online simulations, and adaptive learning platforms that can be customized to each student's skill level and progress. These resources enable teachers to personalize instruction more efficiently and provide immediate feedback, helping students stay motivated and on track.

Ultimately, differentiated instruction not only enhances student engagement but also builds a culture of respect for individual differences. By valuing and accommodating diverse learning styles, teachers empower students to embrace their unique strengths, overcome challenges, and take an active role in their education. This approach cultivates confidence, independence, and a lifelong enthusiasm for learning.

Creating Relevance and Connection: Making learning relevant to students' lives is a powerful strategy for capturing their interest and reducing resistance. When students see how academic content connects to their own experiences, the real world, or their future aspirations, they are more likely to engage actively and develop a genuine interest in the subject. Relevance provides context and meaning, transforming abstract concepts into practical knowledge that students can relate to and use beyond the classroom.

One way to create relevance is by linking lessons to real-world applications. For example, math concepts can be tied to budgeting, architecture, or engineering, while science lessons can explore pressing environmental issues or innovations in technology. Social studies and literature can be connected to current events or cultural phenomena, helping students see the relevance of these subjects in understanding the world around them. These connections make learning tangible and demonstrate the value of academic skills in solving everyday problems or contributing to society.

Teachers can also make learning personal by connecting content to students' individual interests, hobbies, and experiences. For instance, a student passionate about music might analyze song lyrics to understand literary devices, while a sports enthusiast could explore statistics and probability through game analytics. Allowing students to incorporate their unique perspectives into assignments fosters a sense of ownership and personal investment in their learning.

Additionally, framing lessons within the context of students' future aspirations can inspire them to engage with the material. Discussing how a subject relates to potential career paths or life goals helps students understand its long-term importance. For example, demonstrating how communication skills learned in English class will benefit them in job interviews or professional settings can motivate students to hone their abilities.

By consistently demonstrating the relevance of academic content, teachers not only capture students' attention but also help them develop a deeper appreciation for learning. This approach fosters curiosity, motivation, and a willingness to engage with challenging material, ultimately empowering students to connect their education with their lives and ambitions in meaningful ways.

Promoting Collaborative Learning: Collaborative activities provide students with invaluable opportunities to learn from and inspire one another. By working together in a shared environment, students can exchange ideas, clarify concepts, and support each other in ways that extend beyond traditional instruction. From the start of each school year, I emphasize the importance of collaboration in my classroom, actively encouraging students to help one another whenever possible. I firmly believe that peer interaction fosters a deeper understanding of the material, as students often explain concepts in ways that are more accessible and relatable to their classmates. For example, if students are struggling with a particular math problem and I am unable to address their question immediately, they know they can seek assistance from a peer who may have a better grasp of the concept. This approach not only helps students feel more confident in seeking help, but it also encourages them to take ownership of their learning.

To further enhance this collaborative spirit, I make it a point to recognize and reward students who engage in peer tutoring during class periods. This can involve Carpenter Cash, giving points towards participation grades, or highlighting the value of their contributions in front of the class. Rewarding peer tutoring not only reinforces the importance of helping others but also motivates students to take on leadership roles and deepen their own understanding of the material. These acts of collaboration go beyond simple assistance; they cultivate a classroom culture where cooperation, mutual respect, and active engagement are paramount.

Group work and projects are also key elements in fostering a collaborative environment. When students collaborate on tasks, they not only encourage each other to think critically and creatively but also develop essential interpersonal skills. Through working together, students learn to navigate different perspectives, resolve conflicts, and communicate effectively. This approach nurtures a sense of shared achievement, where success is not only individual but collective. It is through these group experiences that students develop a strong sense of camaraderie, where initial reluctance often transforms into active participation and a willingness to engage. Collaborative learning truly enriches the classroom, creating an environment where every student can contribute and benefit from the collective knowledge and strengths of their peers.

Celebrating Achievements and Progress

Recognizing and celebrating milestones not only boosts student confidence but also reinforces the motivation to continue striving towards bigger goals. Celebrations in learning can mirror the rewards in sports, where achievements, both big and small, are acknowledged with recognition and praise.

Encouraging Self-Reflection: Encouraging self-reflection is an essential part of fostering student growth and celebrating progress. When I tell a student, "Wow, you've come a long way this year," the immediate smile on their face demonstrates the powerful impact of acknowledging their achievements. This simple yet meaningful encouragement serves as a catalyst for deeper self-reflection. It's my hope that such moments inspire students to take a step back and evaluate their journey, recognizing how far they've come and understanding the effort it took to get there.

Self-reflection allows students to analyze their strengths, identify areas for improvement, and set realistic goals for continued growth. This process helps them see learning as a journey, rather than a destination. Implementing self-reflection activities, such as journaling or end-of-week reflections, provides students with structured opportunities to think critically about their academic progress and personal development. For example, asking students to write about a challenge they recently overcame in class or a skill they've improved upon can help solidify the value of persistence and effort.

Moreover, self-reflection builds intrinsic motivation. When students take ownership of their learning and accomplishments, they're more likely to set ambitious goals and actively pursue them. Teachers can support this by offering positive reinforcement and constructive feedback that encourages students to continue striving. Celebrating progress through self-reflection also fosters resilience, as students learn to view setbacks not as failures but as opportunities for growth.

By encouraging self-reflection, educators empower students to take pride in their achievements and develop a sense of agency over their learning journey. This practice not only motivates students to excel academically but also instills lifelong skills of self-awareness, goal setting, and perseverance, preparing them for success beyond the classroom.

Building a Supportive Community: Celebrations are more impactful when shared with others, and this principle is at the heart of creating a positive and nurturing classroom environment. I believe that a classroom should be more than just a space for academic learning; it should also be a community where students feel valued, supported, and encouraged to succeed. By incorporating positive reinforcement into my daily teaching practice, I create an atmosphere where students are motivated to continue striving for excellence. Simple acts of acknowledgment, such as verbal praise, small rewards, or public recognition, help students feel seen and appreciated for their hard work and dedication. These celebrations, no matter how small, contribute to a culture of positivity that fuels student engagement and confidence.

In addition to individual recognition, it is essential to foster a classroom community where peer recognition and collaborative achievements are not only accepted but actively encouraged. I encourage students to recognize each other's successes, whether big or small, and to celebrate the contributions of their classmates. This peer recognition is crucial in building a sense of belonging and unity among students, where they understand that everyone's success is intertwined with the success of the group. When students are celebrated for their accomplishments by their peers, it reinforces the idea that they are part of a larger support system where everyone is rooting for one another.

This supportive classroom community creates a sense of camaraderie that drives students to push their limits and reach new heights. The progress of their peers often serves as inspiration, motivating students to strive for excellence and improve their own performance. When students witness the success of those around them, they realize that growth and progress are possible for everyone, and this shared journey creates an environment where success is not just an individual pursuit, but a collective one. In such a community, students are empowered to reach their fullest potential, knowing that they are supported and encouraged every step of the way.

Recognizing Effort over Outcome: While achievements are certainly important markers of success, it is equally vital to place emphasis on the effort and perseverance that students demonstrate throughout their learning journey. Too often, the focus in education is placed solely on the final outcomes, such as grades or test scores, without recognizing the hard work and commitment required to achieve those results. By highlighting effort, teachers can reinforce the idea that the process of learning is just as valuable as the end result, and that growth comes not only from success but from the willingness to work through challenges and setbacks.

When teachers prioritize effort, they create an environment where students feel supported and encouraged to take risks, make mistakes, and learn from them. This approach helps alleviate the fear of failure, allowing students to embrace the learning process as a valuable experience in itself, regardless of the outcome. By recognizing and praising their dedication, teachers reassure students that persistence is a key factor in achieving success. This shift in focus helps students build resilience, as they come to understand that progress is not always linear, but rather, it is achieved through continuous effort and a determination to improve.

In a classroom that values effort, students are motivated to set personal goals and push themselves beyond their comfort zones. Instead of feeling discouraged by a temporary setback or a less-than-perfect result, they understand that growth is attainable through consistent hard work. Teachers who celebrate effort foster a mindset of perseverance, where students learn to value the journey of learning itself, rather than just the destination. Over time, this mindset helps students develop a sense of self-efficacy, as they recognize that their success is largely within their control, and their hard work is the key to overcoming obstacles and achieving their goals. By acknowledging effort, teachers not only inspire students to work harder but also help them develop a growth mindset that will serve them well beyond the classroom.

Fostering Lifelong Learners

Instilling the motivation to learn in students goes beyond their current academic pursuits to lay the foundation for lifelong learning. I constantly look for ways to help my students see the need for lifelong learning, encouraging them to understand that education does not end with the completion of a course or graduation. Instead, it is an ongoing process that shapes their personal and professional growth. Motivated learners are not only more likely to excel in their academic endeavors but are also better equipped to adapt to new information, embrace change, and navigate the challenges they encounter throughout their lives. In today's world, where technology and industries evolve rapidly, the ability to learn new skills and concepts continuously is crucial. Motivated students understand that learning is a tool for staying relevant, resilient, and engaged in an ever-changing society. As educators, we play a pivotal role in nurturing these qualities by fostering curiosity, providing opportunities for exploration, and encouraging a growth mindset. By acting as coaches, teachers help students set goals, reflect on their progress, and develop the discipline needed to persevere through obstacles. We inspire them to see the value of learning as not just an academic requirement but as a lifelong journey that will continue to enrich their lives.

Encouraging Curiosity and Exploration: Promoting curiosity as a driving force behind learning entices students to explore subjects beyond the curriculum, driven by genuine interest and enthusiasm. In my algebra class, I make a point of being honest with my students and tell them that, in life, they will probably not be using linear equations on a day-to-day basis. However, I also stress that the value of algebra lies not in its immediate, practical application, but in the skills it helps to develop—critical thinking, problem-solving, and the ability to approach unfamiliar situations methodically. To make this more relatable, I often share a fun, hypothetical scenario: if a zombie apocalypse happened and all technology was wiped out, the concepts of algebra (finding an unknown from the known) would be incredibly valuable. Whether it's calculating food supplies, creating strategies for survival, or finding patterns in an unpredictable world, the foundational skills of algebra would become indispensable. This light-hearted approach grabs their attention and encourages them to think beyond the numbers in front of them, fostering a sense of relevance even in seemingly abstract concepts.

By encouraging inquiry-based learning and curiosity-driven projects, teachers can cultivate self-motivated learners who seek knowledge spontaneously. Instead of simply delivering content, I provide opportunities for students to ask questions and explore topics that intrigue them. For example, in group projects or individual assignments, I encourage students to relate algebraic concepts to real-world situations, allowing them to investigate areas that pique their interest. This type of exploration not only makes learning more engaging but also teaches students how to apply their knowledge in creative ways. Over time, this approach helps students develop a deeper connection to the material, as they realize that learning is not just about memorizing formulas or passing tests, but about developing a mindset of exploration and discovery. When curiosity drives learning, students become more independent and self-directed, eager to seek out new knowledge for its own sake. Ultimately, this approach not only enhances their academic success but also sets the foundation for lifelong learning.

Instilling Confidence and Agency: Empowering students with the confidence and agency to take charge of their education fosters signs of autonomy and responsibility that are crucial for their academic and personal growth. By providing students with opportunities to lead their learning, teachers can help them develop the skills needed to succeed not only in the classroom but in life. In my 8th-grade math class, I make it a priority to build this sense of agency from the very beginning of a lesson. When introducing a new concept, I always start with the most basic elements of the objective, ensuring that everyone has a solid understanding of the foundational principles before moving to the more complex aspects. This gradual approach allows students to build their confidence step by step, which is key to their sense of accomplishment.

Once we practice the concept as a class, and I see that most, if not all, of the students grasp the process, I like to inject a bit of humor into the situation by sarcastically saying, "8th-grade math is so hard." They often respond with something like, "No, it's not. This is easy!" While the concept we're covering may, in fact, be quite complex, their response indicates a newfound sense of mastery and confidence. This shift in mindset is crucial students who once may have been intimidated by math now approach it with a sense of capability, believing in their ability to conquer challenges. In a subject like math, where students often struggle with anxiety around their abilities, seeing them overcome obstacles fosters a positive self-image and a more resilient attitude toward learning.

As they witness the impact of their efforts, learners become more prepared to engineer their paths, crossing hurdles in education and beyond. When students feel confident in their abilities, they are more likely to take risks, ask questions, and actively seek opportunities for growth. This confidence translates into agency—the belief that they have control over their learning and that their efforts have tangible results. It's this sense of agency that empowers students to take initiative, set their own goals, and pursue challenges with the mindset that they are capable of succeeding. Ultimately, when students develop confidence and agency, they not only become stronger learners but also gain the skills they need to navigate an ever-changing world.

Emphasizing Adaptability and Critical Thinking: The ability to think critically and adapt to new situations and challenges remains pivotal in an increasingly dynamic world. As our world continues to change rapidly, students need to develop not just knowledge, but also the skills to assess, analyze, and apply information effectively in varying contexts. In my classroom, I place a strong emphasis on cultivating critical thinking, encouraging students to not only answer questions but to deeply understand the reasoning behind their answers. To do this, I ask many "Why?" questions, which challenge students to think beyond surface-level responses and consider the underlying principles or causes that inform their answers. This strategy helps them engage more deeply with the material, fostering a mindset where they actively reflect on their thinking and the logic behind it.

For example, after a student answers an easier knowledge or comprehension question correctly, I often follow up by asking, "That is exactly right. Why is that the answer?" This approach requires students to articulate their reasoning, which encourages them to make connections between different concepts and solidify their understanding. It also encourages them to explore alternative viewpoints and solutions, rather than simply memorizing information. By asking these "Why?" questions, I help students develop the habit of thinking critically about the material and the world around them.

Encouraging students to develop these skills prepares them for a future where change is inevitable, ensuring they remain lifelong learners capable of thriving amidst uncertainties. In a world where technology, industries, and societal needs are constantly evolving, the ability to adapt and think critically will serve them well. They will be better equipped to solve problems, make informed decisions, and approach challenges with confidence. This preparation is essential not only for academic success but also for navigating an unpredictable future.

Conclusion: Honoring the Coach-Student Dynamic

Drawing inspiration from Tom Landry's wisdom, I embrace the role of a coach with determination and purpose. Just as a great coach nurtures the unique potential of each player, I strive to advocate for my students, guiding them to uncover and achieve their goals, even in the face of challenges. Being a teacher-coach means seeing each student as an individual with untapped potential, understanding their strengths and areas of growth, and creating a supportive environment where they feel empowered to thrive.

This approach begins with building trust and cultivating relationships rooted in mutual respect. By taking the time to truly understand my students' needs, aspirations, and fears, I can create a classroom culture that values growth, effort, and perseverance. I aim to equip my students with the skills and mindset necessary to navigate obstacles, transforming setbacks into steppingstones toward success. Motivation and resilience aren't just qualities I hope to instill in my students; they are the pillars upon which my teaching philosophy is built.

In this role, my central objective remains unwavering: to inspire students to engage deeply and passionately with the world of knowledge. This means fostering curiosity, encouraging critical thinking, and helping students see learning as a lifelong adventure. Whether we're solving algebraic equations, exploring real-world applications of math, or reflecting on personal growth, my goal is to make every lesson an opportunity for discovery and connection.

I believe that education is not just about transmitting information but about sparking transformation. When students feel supported, valued, and challenged, they develop the confidence to take risks and the drive to pursue their dreams. By serving as their coach, I am committed to helping them not only succeed academically but also grow into resilient, curious, and empowered individuals who are ready to make their mark on the world. In every student's journey, I strive to be the coach who encourages them to see their potential, rise above limitations, and embrace the joy of learning.

Reflection and Action Step

What is one way I can encourage students who feel discouraged or lack confidence in my subject area to see their potential for growth?

How can I make learning activities more engaging for students who are not naturally interested in the material?

What specific steps can I take to help students set and achieve realistic learning goals in my classroom?

How will I recognize and celebrate student effort and progress, not just final achievement?

What strategies can I use to help students overcome negative beliefs about their abilities, such as "I'm just not a math person"?

Action Step

At the start of a new unit, have each student set a personal learning goal related to the subject (e.g., mastering a specific math concept or improving their test score). Frame the learning process as a journey toward achieving something meaningful to them. Regularly remind students that, like athletes coached to push beyond their comfort zones, they are working toward their own aspirations—even when the work feels challenging. Use encouraging, coaching-style language to reinforce that overcoming difficulties is part of reaching their goals.

Chapter 2 - Prioritizing Learners over Personal Comfort

In education, the student must always remain at the heart of the process, with their needs, aspirations, and journey toward knowledge and growth taking precedence. While teachers inevitably bring their unique experiences, personalities, and teaching styles to the classroom, true success in education lies in prioritizing the learner's experience above the educator's comfort or preferences. This chapter delves into the concept that "My Learning Style and Comfort Level is Not Important," emphasizing that teaching is not merely a profession but an ethical, moral, and contractual commitment to nurturing student development.

I often reflect on my own learning style, which falls into a minority group that represents only 6% of learners. This recognition has led me to acknowledge that if I were a student in my own class, I might have struggled. My classroom, tailored to accommodate the majority learning style—representing 94% of learners—is designed to serve a diverse student body rather than my own preferences. This realization reinforces the necessity of adaptability in teaching, ensuring that all students feel supported, understood, and empowered to succeed.

Effective teaching requires educators to step outside their comfort zones and embrace strategies that cater to the varied learning needs of their students. It demands empathy to understand different perspectives, dedication to refining instructional methods, and flexibility to adjust to changing dynamics in the classroom. By doing so, teachers create an equitable learning environment where every student, regardless of their background or learning style, can thrive.

Ultimately, the role of a teacher is not about imposing their preferred methods but about crafting a learning experience that uplifts and engages every individual in the classroom. When educators prioritize students' needs over their own, they foster a culture of inclusion, innovation, and genuine connection—hallmarks of a truly transformative educational experience.

Shifting the Focus: It's Not About Me

Effective education begins with shifting the traditional view of what it means to teach. The principle "it's not about me" serves as a powerful reminder that the classroom is a space dedicated to learners and their growth, not a platform for instructors to showcase their comfort zones or preferred methods. While my personal learning style and preferences undoubtedly shape my teaching approach, they must not dominate or limit the opportunities available to the diverse array of students in my classroom. Every teaching decision I make should stem from a conscious effort to prioritize the varied needs, interests, and learning styles of my students.

Teaching is not a reflection of what I find comfortable or intuitive; rather, it is about what actively engages students, deepens their comprehension, and paves the way for their success. As an educator, my responsibility is to move beyond personal biases and preferences, instead focusing on strategies that address the needs of all learners— whether they excel through visual aids, auditory instruction, reading and writing activities, or hands-on experiences. This requires creativity, adaptability, and an ongoing commitment to refine my methods to meet the evolving demands of my students.

To achieve this, I regularly evaluate my teaching practices, seeking input from students, colleagues, and even parents to identify areas for growth. Incorporating varied instructional techniques and tools ensures that I reach every learner, empowering them to engage with content in a way that resonates with their strengths. For example, incorporating group discussions, multimedia presentations, and interactive activities allows students to explore material from multiple angles, enhancing both understanding and retention.

When I step outside my comfort zone to adapt to the needs of my students, I model resilience and a growth mindset, demonstrating that learning and improvement are lifelong endeavors. By doing so, I foster a classroom culture where diversity in learning is celebrated, challenges are embraced, and every student feels seen and valued. Ultimately, this commitment to inclusivity and adaptability creates a dynamic learning environment where students are not just educated but inspired to reach their full potential.

The Ethical and Moral Dimensions of Teaching

Education is far more than the transfer of information; it is a profound ethical and moral engagement that shapes how individuals understand themselves and interact with the world. As an educator, my ethics and morals demand that I never "phone it in." Instead, I must actively strive to be the best teacher I can be. This commitment involves a deep sense of responsibility to provide equitable access to education, addressing the systemic barriers and inequities students may face. Teaching is a profession that requires vigilance, adaptability, and an unwavering dedication to each student's growth and success.

A crucial aspect of this ethical responsibility is the recognition and mitigation of potential biases, which can unconsciously influence how we engage with students. Implementing culturally relevant pedagogy—approaches that honor and reflect students' unique identities and experiences—is key to fostering an inclusive and affirming classroom environment. By aligning curriculum and teaching methods to accommodate learners of diverse abilities, languages, and cultural backgrounds, educators create spaces where students feel seen, respected, and valued. This sense of belonging enhances active participation and mutual respect, laying the groundwork for deeper learning.

The moral foundation of teaching also involves embracing inclusivity and differentiation. Providing tailored resources and interventions for students who need extra support—or challenging those ready for advanced work—underscores the importance of meeting each learner where they are. This approach is not just about fairness; it is about empowerment, equipping students with the confidence and tools they need to succeed in their educational journey and beyond.

Ultimately, teaching is a moral contract rooted in the belief that every student deserves the opportunity to thrive. By upholding these values, educators help bridge gaps, inspire potential, and guide students toward futures shaped by possibility and achievement. This commitment transforms the classroom into a space of equity, empowerment, and meaningful growth.

Legal and Contractual Accountability

Teaching duties are also framed by explicit legal and contractual expectations. Within curricular mandates, educators must align lessons with state and federal standards and adhere to institutional protocols. These aspects form the foundation of an educator's contractual obligations, ensuring educational integrity, consistency, and accountability.

Staying compliant while being malleable may appear challenging; however, forward-thinking educators recognize that fulfilling legal requirements need not mean compromising the responsivity to student needs. Instead, pathways emerge for reconciling curricular standards and innovative, context-tailored instruction, thus bridging the gap between formal stipulations and fostering personal, relevant learning.

Furthermore, law often dictates inclusive practices, like individualized education program (IEP) accommodations for students with diverse learning needs or the adherence to ESL protocols for non-native speakers. Effective educators develop a rich understanding of each student's educational context and leverage laws to support unique learner success. Abiding by these regulations ensures that I honor my commitments—and reaffirm that student-centered, adaptive instruction is feasible and necessary under legal frameworks.

Challenging Comfort and Adapting to Student Needs

Placing learners at the center of education necessitates that teachers consistently surpass the constraints of comfort zones, initiating growth and evolution in their practice. Education constantly evolves alongside society, with new curricula, technologies, and pedagogical approaches establishing transformative possibilities within classrooms.

As teachers chart these shifts, continuous, relevant professional development becomes indispensable. Embracing learning opportunities—in technology integration, differentiated instruction, or student mental health—equips educators to instruct with newfound creativity and relevance. This dynamic transformation offers a living example to students that learning is a resilient, endless venture, one that requires dedication and openness to change.

This teaching philosophy requires teachers to actively listen and gather feedback from learners. Techniques such as surveys, informal conversations, and reflective exercises can unveil how students perceive their experiences, guiding educators in fine-tuning their approaches to address any issues and replicate successes. After all, a willingness to adapt further underscores a teacher's commitment to a learning environment conducive to student growth.

Conclusion: Cultivating a Learner-Centric Community

"My Learning Style and Comfort Level is Not Important" represents a transformative approach to education, emphasizing authentic, meaningful engagement that prioritizes the needs, struggles, and aspirations of students. This philosophy challenges educators to move beyond their own preferences and embrace the diversity of learning styles and experiences that students bring to the classroom. Rooted in ethical, moral, legal, and contractual responsibilities, effective teaching demands discernment: understanding each child's unique resources and leveraging them to cultivate active, capable learners. When educators lead with empathy, creativity, and innovation, they create inclusive and supportive environments where equity is not just an abstract ideal but a practiced reality.

An impactful teacher is one who evolves alongside their students, continuously seeking and refining strategies that help learners excel. This evolution involves listening, adapting, and pushing beyond the familiar to address the dynamic needs of a diverse classroom. It requires the courage to challenge traditional norms and the commitment to celebrate every student's potential. By fostering a culture of inclusivity, mutual respect, and curiosity, teachers empower students to discover their strengths, confront challenges with resilience, and envision broader possibilities for their future.

Teaching extends far beyond the transmission of knowledge—it is a moral calling to shape individuals who are not only skilled but also compassionate and driven. It is about creating a community where learners feel valued and inspired to contribute meaningfully to the world. In this vision, education becomes a shared journey of growth and discovery, fostering a legacy of understanding and ambition.

Ultimately, this mindset transforms classrooms into spaces of empowerment and connection, where both teachers and students are partners in the pursuit of growth. It challenges educators to reimagine their roles and reminds us all that impactful teaching is built on a foundation of equity, empathy, and a steadfast belief in the potential of every learner. Together, we forge a path toward a future shaped by compassion, innovation, and boundless opportunity.

Reflection and Action Step

How can I adjust my teaching methods to better meet the diverse learning needs of my students, even if it means stepping outside my own comfort zone?

What is one way I can ensure that students with different learning styles feel supported and included in my classroom?

How do I check that my lesson plans are focused on student growth rather than my own preferred teaching style?

When have I noticed my personal comfort influencing my teaching decisions, and how can I shift my focus back to student needs?

What strategies can I try to better understand the perspectives and challenges faced by students whose learning styles differ from my own?

How will I know if my classroom environment is truly equitable and responsive to all learners, and what steps can I take to improve it if needed?

Action Step

Dedicate time each week to offer students a choice in how they demonstrate their understanding of key concepts. For example, after a lesson, allow students to select from multiple project formats (such as a written report, visual presentation, creative video, or hands-on model). This approach ensures that students with different learning styles and strengths feel valued and supported, even if it requires you to adapt your usual teaching routines or grading methods. By prioritizing student preferences and needs over personal comfort, you create a more inclusive and engaging classroom environment that fosters growth for all learners.

Chapter 3 - The Importance of Adopting a Philosophy of Education

Defining and adopting a personal philosophy of education is fundamental to becoming an effective and transformative educator. In the ever-changing landscape of the modern world, education serves as one of the most vital pillars of societal advancement and individual empowerment. It shapes how people understand themselves, their communities, and their potential contributions to a global society. As the conduit through which knowledge, skills, and values are passed from one generation to the next, education must be guided by a philosophy that not only addresses the needs of learners today but also prepares them for the complexities of tomorrow.

A philosophy of education acts as a guiding framework, grounding an educator's decisions in principles that ensure intentionality and purpose. It informs pedagogical methods, curriculum design, and the way educators engage with students. Without such a philosophy, teaching risks becoming transactional, focused solely on meeting immediate objectives rather than fostering deeper understanding, critical thinking, and lifelong curiosity. A well-defined philosophy of education, by contrast, allows teachers to align their work with a broader vision that values equity, inclusivity, and the holistic development of every student.

This philosophy is not static; it evolves alongside the educator, shaped by experiences in the classroom, advances in educational research, and the changing needs of society. For instance, in today's interconnected and technology-driven world, a philosophy of education might emphasize the importance of digital literacy, global awareness, and adaptability. It might also advocate for culturally responsive teaching that recognizes and respects the diverse backgrounds and perspectives students bring to the classroom.

Moreover, a strong educational philosophy empowers educators to create learning environments where students feel valued, supported, and challenged. It prioritizes meaningful and equitable learning experiences that cater to varied learning styles, needs, and aspirations. By placing the student at the center of the educational process, educators foster not just academic growth but also the social, emotional, and moral development necessary for thriving in a complex world.

Ultimately, adopting a philosophy of education is not merely an academic exercise—it is a moral and professional commitment to excellence in teaching. It is the foundation for building classrooms that inspire curiosity, encourage resilience, and nurture the potential of every learner. In doing so, educators contribute to a more informed, empathetic, and empowered society, fulfilling the profound promise of education as a force for positive change.

Defining a Philosophy of Education

A philosophy of education encompasses a set of beliefs and values about the purpose, process, nature, and ideal content of education. It serves as a blueprint for how educators view their roles, define learning, and engage with students, shaping their approach to the complex and dynamic task of teaching. A well-articulated philosophy answers fundamental questions: Why do we educate? What is the role of the teacher? How should learning be experienced? It reflects the educator's understanding of their mission to prepare students not only for academic success but also for responsible citizenship, personal fulfillment, and lifelong learning.

By defining a philosophy of education, educators establish a framework that provides consistent guidance across the myriad challenges and decisions encountered in the teaching process. This framework ensures that every choice—whether it's selecting curriculum materials, designing assessments, or managing classroom interactions—is aligned with a clear vision and purpose. Without such a foundation, educational practices can become fragmented and reactive, failing to serve the holistic needs of students or the broader demands of society.

A philosophy of education also helps teachers balance the dual imperatives of maintaining academic rigor and fostering a supportive, inclusive learning environment. It allows them to articulate how they view the role of the teacher—not as a mere conveyor of information but as a guide, mentor, and facilitator who helps students uncover their potential and build critical thinking skills. It emphasizes the importance of creating learning experiences that are engaging, meaningful, and connected to students' lives and future aspirations.

Furthermore, a well-defined philosophy of education promotes adaptability in the face of change. As society evolves, so too must educational approaches. Whether integrating technology, responding to cultural shifts, or addressing new research on how students learn, educators with a strong philosophy are better equipped to embrace innovation while staying true to their core principles.

Defining a philosophy of education is not solely for the benefit of the educator; it directly impacts students. A teacher with a clear educational philosophy can communicate expectations, values, and goals effectively, creating a classroom culture where students understand the "why" behind their learning journey. This transparency fosters trust, motivation, and a sense of purpose among students, empowering them to take ownership of their education.

In the absence of a guiding philosophy, teaching risks becoming transactional—a series of disconnected tasks that fail to inspire or engage. A coherent philosophy, however, transforms education into a meaningful process that cultivates intellectual curiosity, personal growth, and a commitment to lifelong learning. By defining their philosophy, educators not only enhance their teaching but also contribute to a more equitable, informed, and compassionate society.

Clarifying Purpose and Goals

One of the most significant benefits of adopting a philosophy of education is the clarity it provides in defining educational purpose and goals. A clearly articulated philosophy helps educators establish what education should achieve in broad, visionary terms, while also enabling them to set specific, actionable objectives within their classrooms or institutions. For instance, an educator who embraces a progressivist philosophy may focus on cultivating critical thinking, encouraging problem-solving, and fostering collaboration among students. Their goals might center on preparing students to adapt to an ever-changing world and contribute creatively to society. On the other hand, an educator who aligns with an essentialist philosophy might prioritize mastery of core academic subjects such as mathematics, science, and literature, emphasizing foundational skills as the bedrock of intellectual development.

This clarity in purpose serves as a guiding compass for educators, ensuring that every aspect of their teaching practice aligns with their overarching goals. Decisions about curriculum content, instructional methods, and assessment strategies are no longer arbitrary or reactive but become intentional and purpose-driven. For example, a progressivist teacher might incorporate project-based learning and group activities to foster collaboration, while an essentialist teacher might design structured lessons with clear benchmarks to reinforce foundational knowledge.

The benefits of this alignment are far-reaching. It allows educators to create a coherent and integrated learning experience where each lesson, activity, and evaluation contributes meaningfully to the students' growth. Students, in turn, are more likely to find purpose in their education, as they can see how individual lessons connect to larger learning objectives and their personal aspirations.

Moreover, clarifying educational goals fosters consistency across an institution or school system. When educators share and implement a unified vision, it becomes easier to establish benchmarks, evaluate progress, and provide targeted support where needed. For instance, a school emphasizing social and emotional learning might adopt goals that prioritize empathy, resilience, and interpersonal skills, ensuring these values are reflected in classroom practices, extracurricular activities, and staff training.

Finally, a well-defined philosophy of education can inspire reflection and adaptability. As societal needs evolve, educators can revisit their philosophy to ensure it remains relevant and effective. For example, the rise of digital literacy and global interconnectedness may prompt educators to integrate new technologies and multicultural perspectives into their teaching.

In clarifying purpose and goals, a philosophy of education transforms teaching into a purposeful, impactful practice. It provides a foundation that not only informs day-to-day decisions but also inspires long-term commitment to nurturing well-rounded, capable, and motivated learners.

By grounding their practice in a clear philosophy, educators are better equipped to create dynamic and effective learning environments. This philosophy serves as a framework that guides decision-making and fosters consistency in teaching practices. For example, an educator who values experiential learning may prioritize hands-on activities and real-world problem-solving tasks, while a teacher who emphasizes mastery of content might focus on direct instruction and incremental skill-building. These methodologies are not mutually exclusive, but the philosophy behind them determines how they are integrated into classroom practice.

Moreover, a well-articulated philosophy of education empowers teachers to navigate challenges and adapt to evolving educational contexts. As technological advancements reshape the learning landscape and societal needs evolve, educators who anchor their practice in foundational principles can embrace change without losing sight of their core objectives. For example, a teacher whose philosophy emphasizes the development of critical thinking skills might incorporate digital tools like online simulations or virtual discussions to enhance student engagement while staying true to their educational values.

This guiding philosophy also supports reflective practice, encouraging teachers to assess and refine their approaches continually. When educators understand the "why" behind their methods, they are more likely to evaluate their effectiveness and make informed adjustments. This adaptability is crucial in addressing diverse student needs and fostering inclusive learning environments.

Ultimately, a thoughtful philosophy of education not only informs teaching methodologies but also inspires educators to remain passionate about their work. It serves as a source of motivation, reminding them of their purpose in shaping the lives of their students and contributing to a better future. Whether emphasizing creativity, critical thinking, or collaboration, a strong educational philosophy ensures that teaching remains a meaningful and impactful endeavor.

Fostering a Supportive Learning Environment

A well-articulated philosophy of education plays a pivotal role in fostering a supportive and empowering learning environment. My personal philosophy is simple and straightforward yet profound: "teaching is causing to learn." This belief shapes my approach, ensuring I create an environment where students are free to learn in ways that align with their unique styles and preferences. Such a philosophy not only guides the teacher but also profoundly impacts the attitudes and beliefs of students. It establishes a foundation for mutual respect, promotes diversity, encourages inclusiveness, and prioritizes personal development.

An educational philosophy rooted in core principles like humanism emphasizes the emotional wellbeing, individual development, and self-fulfillment of students. Humanism centers on the intrinsic value of each learner and fosters a learning environment where empathy, understanding, and respect are paramount. In such an atmosphere, students' voices are not only heard but deeply valued. Teachers act as facilitators, guiding learners to grow both intellectually and emotionally. By prioritizing personal growth alongside academic achievement, educators help students develop a holistic sense of self.

For example, a classroom guided by a humanistic philosophy would promote active listening, open dialogue, and collaboration. Teachers would celebrate diverse perspectives, ensuring each student feels acknowledged and appreciated. When students experience this level of care and consistency, they are more likely to feel safe and understood. This, in turn, nurtures a positive learning environment where curiosity thrives, and students feel empowered to take risks in their education.

Furthermore, a well-defined philosophy of education provides clarity and direction in handling challenges. When educators consistently apply their values, they create a predictable and fair environment that students can rely on. This predictability fosters trust and reinforces the importance of integrity and accountability. By embedding values like respect, inclusiveness, and empathy into daily practice, teachers can address conflicts constructively and maintain a harmonious classroom dynamic.

In essence, a thoughtful educational philosophy transforms the classroom into more than just a place of instruction. It becomes a community where every individual is encouraged to learn, grow, and contribute meaningfully. Through clear principles and compassionate practices, teachers cultivate environments that inspire lifelong learning and equip students with the skills they need to succeed both academically and personally.

Addressing Societal Needs

Educational philosophy extends far beyond the confines of classroom walls, shaping how education systems respond to and address the pressing needs of society. Today's world is fraught with challenges such as economic disparities, environmental crises, and social injustices. These complex issues demand thoughtful and intentional educational approaches that prepare students to engage with and contribute to solutions. A well-defined philosophy of education provides a framework for integrating these societal concerns into both the curriculum and the broader educational experience.

For instance, an educator aligned with a social reconstructionist philosophy might prioritize critical pedagogy that empowers students to analyze and question societal norms. This approach encourages learners to identify and address injustices while envisioning pathways for meaningful change. Education, in this context, becomes a powerful tool for empowerment—a means of fostering informed, ethical citizens who are equipped to contribute to the collective betterment of society. By engaging students in discussions about equity, sustainability, and social responsibility, educators can inspire them to become active participants in shaping a more just and sustainable world.

Moreover, a philosophy of education rooted in addressing societal needs often emphasizes interdisciplinary learning and real-world application. For example, integrating environmental science with community service projects can help students understand the practical implications of sustainability while contributing to local conservation efforts. Similarly, teaching financial literacy and entrepreneurship within the context of economic disparities can prepare students to navigate and influence the economic landscape more effectively. These approaches ensure that education remains relevant and responsive to societal needs.

Educational philosophy also underscores the importance of equity and access in learning opportunities. By advocating for inclusive practices and recognizing the diverse backgrounds and experiences of students, educators can work toward reducing systemic barriers and promoting social mobility. This commitment to equity not only benefits individual learners but also strengthens communities and societies as a whole.

In conclusion, a robust philosophy of education equips schools and educators to address societal challenges proactively and thoughtfully. By fostering critical thinking, ethical reasoning, and a sense of social responsibility, education can empower individuals to contribute to the creation of a more equitable and sustainable future. In this way, educational philosophy serves as a guiding force for both individual growth and collective progress.

Empowering Educators for Professional Growth

Adopting a robust philosophy of education plays a transformative role in an educator's professional growth and development. By reflecting on their personal beliefs and values, educators are prompted to engage in continuous learning about educational theories, innovative pedagogical strategies, and best practices. A clear and well-defined philosophy serves as an anchor, guiding teachers as they evaluate new ideas and methods in the ever-evolving landscape of education. For instance, I actively seek professional development opportunities and take courses that enable me to implement my philosophy more effectively, ensuring that my teaching remains relevant and impactful.

This commitment to a philosophy of education fosters a mindset of lifelong learning and adaptability among educators. It encourages them to remain open to change, embrace new technologies, and experiment with creative teaching methods. As the needs of students and society evolve, educators with a strong philosophy are better equipped to adapt their approaches while staying true to their core principles. This balance between consistency and flexibility allows teachers to continuously refine their skills and enhance their effectiveness in the classroom.

Moreover, a philosophy of education empowers educators to engage in reflective practice, a cornerstone of professional growth. By regularly assessing their teaching methods and the outcomes of their instruction, teachers can identify areas for improvement and celebrate their successes. Reflection fosters a deeper understanding of one's strengths and challenges, creating opportunities for targeted professional development. For example, an educator who values inclusivity may seek training on differentiated instruction to better meet the diverse needs of their students.

Collaboration is another key aspect of professional growth influenced by an educational philosophy. Teachers who share similar values can work together to exchange ideas, resources, and strategies, fostering a culture of mutual support and innovation. Professional learning communities, peer mentoring, and collaborative workshops become valuable spaces where educators can grow collectively while staying aligned with their shared goals.

Furthermore, a strong philosophy of education inspires educators to take on leadership roles within their schools and communities. By articulating their beliefs and demonstrating their commitment to student success, teachers can influence educational policies, mentor new educators, and contribute to systemic improvements. This sense of purpose and agency not only enhances their professional satisfaction but also amplifies their impact on the broader educational landscape.

In essence, a thoughtful and well-articulated philosophy of education empowers educators to pursue professional growth with intention and enthusiasm. It serves as a guiding light, encouraging lifelong learning, fostering reflective practices, and promoting collaboration and leadership. Through this continuous journey of growth, educators can achieve greater effectiveness, inspire their students, and contribute meaningfully to the advancement of education as a whole.

Conclusion: Towards a Comprehensive Philosophy of Education

In conclusion, adopting a comprehensive philosophy of education is indispensable for creating a purposeful, cohesive, and effective educational experience. It provides clarity of purpose, guides instructional methods, fosters supportive learning environments, addresses societal needs, and propels professional growth among educators. A well-defined philosophy ensures that every aspect of education aligns with the overarching goal of nurturing individuals who can thrive personally and contribute positively to their community.

As the complexities of the world continue to evolve, so must educational practices. A robust philosophy of education equips educators and institutions to rise to these challenges, empowering them to adapt to emerging trends, incorporate innovative technologies, and address the diverse needs of learners. This adaptability is essential for preparing students to navigate an intricate world with confidence, competence, and compassion. For instance, integrating ethical reasoning, critical thinking, and cultural awareness into curricula can help students develop a nuanced understanding of global issues and their roles in creating solutions.

Moreover, a comprehensive philosophy of education encourages a deeper connection between educators, students, and the community. By prioritizing inclusivity, empathy, and collaboration, educational systems can foster environments where all stakeholders feel valued and invested in the learning process. This sense of shared purpose amplifies the impact of education, transforming it into a collective effort to shape a better future.

In essence, an educational philosophy acts as the compass guiding educational systems toward meaningful, lasting impact. It ensures that education fulfills its profound role in shaping individuals and society for future generations. By remaining philosophically driven, educators and institutions can sustain their focus on what truly matters: empowering learners to grow into ethical, informed, and capable citizens who are ready to contribute to a world in constant flux. A philosophy of education is not just a framework—it is a vision for how education can be a force for enduring positive change.

Reflection and Action Step

What core values and beliefs do I want to guide my teaching, and how do these reflect my vision for students' growth and development?

How do I define the purpose of education in today's society, and how does that influence my approach in the classroom?

In what ways can my teaching promote equity, inclusivity, and the holistic development of every student?

How do I ensure that my instructional methods and curriculum design are intentional and aligned with my educational philosophy?

How do I adapt my philosophy as new educational research emerges and as the needs of my students and society change?

How can I recognize and incorporate the diverse backgrounds and perspectives of my students into my teaching?

Action Step

Set aside 30 minutes this week to write a one-paragraph statement summarizing your current philosophy of education. Reflect on the above questions as you write. Then, identify one specific way you can adjust your teaching practice next week to better align with this philosophy—such as incorporating a new inclusive activity, updating a lesson to include digital tools, or inviting students to share their perspectives in class discussions.

Chapter 4 - My Educational Philosophy: Teaching is Causing to Learn

Education is a dynamic process characterized by an intricate interaction between the teacher and the student, a collaborative relationship that lies at the core of meaningful learning. Teaching, in my view, is far more than the mere dissemination of information; it is the facilitation of learning, an active and intentional effort to ignite curiosity, foster understanding, and inspire growth. The phrase "teaching is causing to learn" encapsulates my educational philosophy, reflecting my belief that the ultimate goal of teaching is to ensure that learning occurs. If the student has not learned, then I, as an educator, have not fulfilled my role.

This conviction drives me to assert that there are no "bad" students, only "bad" teachers—a perspective that underscores the profound responsibility educators carry. It is our duty to adapt, innovate, and persevere in our efforts to reach every learner. This philosophy compels me to continually refine my teaching methods, explore diverse strategies, and remain receptive to feedback, ensuring that I meet the unique needs of each student.

Moreover, I view education as a holistic endeavor that extends beyond academic achievement. Effective teaching cultivates critical thinking, emotional intelligence, and a lifelong love of learning. It empowers students to discover their strengths, overcome challenges, and realize their potential. This requires creating a classroom environment that is inclusive, supportive, and conducive to exploration—an environment where every student feels valued and capable.

Ultimately, my teaching philosophy is rooted in the belief that education has the power to transform lives. As an educator, I am committed to fostering not only intellectual growth but also personal and social development. My aim is to equip students with the skills, knowledge, and confidence they need to thrive in an ever-changing world, while instilling in them the belief that learning is a lifelong journey filled with endless possibilities.

Teaching as a Cause for Learning

Teaching is an art, one designed to foster intellectual curiosity, ignite passion, and equip learners with the skills and knowledge required for both personal and societal success. At its essence, teaching must provoke transformation, leading learners beyond rote memorization to genuine understanding and the capacity to apply what they have learned. In this context, the measure of effective teaching is the extent to which students can demonstrate and utilize newfound knowledge.

This philosophy places the learner at the center of the educational process. It requires educators to not only possess a deep understanding of their subject matter but also to be adept at engaging diverse learners. Teaching must accommodate varied learning styles, cognitive abilities, and cultural backgrounds. It demands creativity, flexibility, and empathy from educators, positioning them as facilitators rather than mere transmitters of knowledge.

Challenges of Truly Effective Teaching

Achieving true learning involves overcoming numerous challenges that arise within the educational landscape. Traditional education often emphasizes standardized testing and benchmark assessments, measuring students against uniform criteria. While these assessments can indicate certain levels of proficiency, they frequently fail to capture the nuanced understanding and growth of individual students.

In alignment with my belief that teaching is causing to learn, I advocate for assessment methods that reflect students' ability to apply, interpret, and create based on their learning. These methods could include project-based assignments, collaborative tasks, and real-world problem-solving scenarios, all of which demand deeper cognitive engagement and demonstrate a learner's comprehensive grasp of material.

Additionally, there's the challenge of addressing diverse learning needs. Students do not learn at the same pace, nor do they utilize identical learning strategies. To cause learning effectively, educators must differentiate instruction, tailoring methods and materials to meet varied student needs. This approach calls for innovative educational strategies that embrace technology, inquiry-based learning, and interdisciplinary integration.

Empowering and Engaging Students

One of the cornerstones of my educational philosophy is the belief in empowering students to take ownership of their learning. This empowerment stems from the understanding that students are not empty vessels waiting to be filled with knowledge, but rather dynamic individuals who bring their unique experiences, insights, and questions to the classroom. Acknowledging and valuing these contributions is essential for creating an environment where learning becomes a collaborative and transformative process. Teachers play a pivotal role in cultivating this atmosphere by fostering inclusivity, respect, and encouragement, ensuring every student's voice is heard and appreciated.

A crucial step in this journey is encouraging students to actively engage with the material and their peers. Asking questions, participating in discussions, and even challenging prevailing ideas not only promotes a sense of ownership but also helps students develop confidence in their intellectual abilities. When students feel that their perspectives matter, they are more likely to invest in their education. This shift from passive information receivers to active participants transforms the learning experience, fostering a deeper connection to the subject matter and an intrinsic motivation to explore further.

Empowering students goes beyond academic engagement—it's about equipping them with critical thinking skills, creativity, and a lifelong curiosity. These attributes are essential for navigating an increasingly complex and dynamic world. When students learn to think critically, they become adept at analyzing information, forming reasoned opinions, and making informed decisions. Creativity, on the other hand, allows them to approach problems innovatively, viewing challenges as opportunities for growth rather than obstacles. Curiosity drives them to seek knowledge independently, ensuring their learning doesn't stop at the classroom door.

To truly empower students, educators must adopt a student-centered approach to teaching, where lessons are tailored to meet diverse needs and learning styles. This might include incorporating project-based learning, collaborative activities, and technology-enhanced tools that resonate with students' interests and experiences. Providing constructive feedback and celebrating progress further strengthens students' belief in their potential.

Moreover, fostering a growth mindset in students helps them view failure not as a setback but as a valuable part of the learning process. When students understand that their abilities can be developed through effort and perseverance, they are more likely to embrace challenges and persist in the face of difficulties.

Ultimately, empowering students is about inspiring them to see themselves as capable, resilient, and active learners who can shape their own educational journeys. It's about creating a foundation for lifelong learning, where the pursuit of knowledge becomes a fulfilling and ongoing endeavor.

Reflections on Bad Students vs. Bad Teachers

The assertion that "there are no bad students, only bad teachers" might seem provocative, and offensive to other educators, at first glance, but it challenges us to reconsider the dynamics of education. This perspective is rooted in the belief that students' struggles often reflect systemic deficiencies or ineffective instructional methods rather than inherent shortcomings in the students themselves. Factors such as socio-economic disparities, limited access to resources, undiagnosed learning differences, or uninspired teaching can all hinder a student's academic journey. These external and internal barriers highlight the importance of viewing education through a lens of empathy and adaptability.

Educators carry a significant responsibility to identify and address these challenges effectively. Students who appear disengaged or unmotivated are often responding to a lack of connection between the curriculum and their personal experiences or interests. A responsive teacher works to bridge this gap by employing culturally relevant materials, integrating diverse teaching methods, and linking academic content to real-world scenarios. For example, I strive to make my math class both engaging and enjoyable by implementing a reward system called "Carpenter Cash." Students earn Carpenter Cash for participation, excelling in classroom competitions, helping peers overcome math difficulties, and other positive contributions. This system fosters a lively and collaborative environment while encouraging students to take pride in their efforts. My goal is to create an experience so engaging that students remember it as their most enjoyable math class.

Reflecting on the role of teachers in shaping student outcomes emphasizes the importance of self-assessment, professional growth, and collaboration. Effective educators consistently evaluate their teaching methods, seek feedback from students and peers, and engage in ongoing professional development. These practices enable teachers to adapt their strategies to meet the evolving needs of their students. Moreover, partnering with colleagues, parents, and support specialists can help address diverse learning challenges more comprehensively.

The belief that struggling students are the result of inadequate teaching methods does not absolve students of responsibility but instead highlights the teacher's pivotal role in fostering an environment conducive to success. This perspective inspires educators to continuously refine their craft, ensuring every student has the opportunity to thrive. Ultimately, education is a shared journey, and by addressing barriers to learning with creativity and care, teachers can empower students to overcome obstacles and reach their full potential.

Continuing Teacher Growth

Embracing the philosophy that teaching is causing learning—and there are no bad students, only bad teachers—also demands a commitment to lifelong learning for educators themselves. Teachers should be models of curiosity and growth, showing students that learning is a continuous journey rather than a destination.

Professional development must become an integral and ongoing element of an educator's career. This may include attending workshops, participating in mentorship programs, and engaging in self-directed study of emerging educational methods and philosophies. Such engagement allows educators to remain responsive to innovative pedagogical strategies and global educational shifts, thereby enhancing their teaching effectiveness.

Furthermore, collaboration within learning communities can afford teachers mutual support and idea exchange opportunities, deepen understanding and providing fresh insights into causative teaching strategies. In this manner, educators bolster their own learning journey, ultimately translating these gains into more enriching learning experiences for their students.

Conclusion: Towards an Active Learning

In sum, the view that "teaching is causing to learn" is grounded in a profound commitment to promoting authentic, meaningful, and transformative educational experiences. Teaching exceeds the transmission of information—it is an ongoing process of sparking learners' curiosity, encouraging them to question, explore, and apply their knowledge creatively and critically.

By understanding this intensified responsibility, educators can strive to recognize the potential in every student and effectuate meaningful learning experiences. Consequently, transposing the onus of "failure" from students to ineffective pedagogy and systems insists that educators remain adaptive, compassionate, and eager to improve their practice.

Ultimately, this philosophy recognizes that the essence of education is human growth—not just intellectual attainment—and places the relationship between learner and teacher at its core. By advocating for empathetic, innovative teaching and a collaborative, inclusive classroom environment, this educational philosophy strives to prepare learners who are keen, competent, and equipped to contribute beneficially to the wider society. Such is the transformative power of education: directed not by simplistic measures, but through the intentional and conscientious act of causing genuine learning.

Reflection and Action Step

Based on my philosophy that "teaching is causing to learn," which emphasizes active facilitation, adaptability, student-centered growth, and the transformative power of education:

How do I intentionally design lessons and interactions to ensure that real learning—not just content coverage—occurs for every student?

In what ways am I adapting my teaching strategies to meet the unique needs and learning styles of each student in my classroom?

How do I create a classroom environment where every student feels valued, supported, and empowered to take intellectual risks?

What steps do I take to cultivate curiosity, critical thinking, and a love of learning in my students?

How do I respond when a student is struggling to learn, and what does that reveal about my commitment to their growth?

How am I modeling perseverance, openness to feedback, and lifelong learning in my own professional practice?

In what ways do I foster not only academic achievement but also emotional intelligence and personal development in my students?

Action Step

This week, select one lesson or activity and intentionally redesign it with the explicit goal of "causing to learn"—not just teaching content, but ensuring understanding and engagement for every student. After the lesson, reflect on what worked, what didn't, and how you might further adapt your approach to reach all learners, in line with your philosophy that effective teaching means learning has truly occurred.

My paragraph is: *My teaching philosophy is rooted in the belief that teaching is causing learning. I see my role not as merely delivering information but as creating purposeful experiences that spark curiosity, engage students actively, and lead to lasting understanding. By designing lessons with clear outcomes, adapting to diverse needs, and fostering ownership of learning, I guide students to connect knowledge to their lives and apply it independently. Assessment serves as a tool for growth, while empathy ensures an environment where every learner feels valued. Ultimately, my goal is to be a catalyst for meaningful, lifelong learning.*

Chapter 5 - A Vision for Transformative Education: Servant Leaders in the Classroom

In an era marked by rapid technological advancements and a constantly shifting societal landscape, the field of education faces unprecedented challenges. Educators grapple with an array of issues, from student disengagement to the need for catering to diverse learning requirements. Many students experience a disconnection from the material, struggling to see the relevance of their education in the real world. Teachers find themselves in an uphill battle to maintain interest and motivation in the classroom while ensuring that all learners, regardless of background or ability, are supported and inspired

Amidst these challenges, there is a growing recognition that conventional educational practices may not be sufficient to meet the needs of today's students. This calls for a transformative approach that reimagines the role of educators and the learning environment. Enter the concept of servant leadership—a leadership model wherein the leader prioritizes serving others, empowering them to achieve their highest potential. Robert K. Greenleaf, who introduced the concept in the 1970s, emphasized listening, empathy, and a commitment to the growth of individuals as the core values of servant leadership. When applied in teaching, this model can inspire educators to foster environments where students feel valued, understood, and motivated to learn.

The relevance of servant leadership in the classroom cannot be overstated. At its heart, it shifts the focus from a teacher-centric model—which often emphasizes authority and control—to a learner-centric model. Here, my job as an educator is to act as a facilitator of knowledge, mentor, and guide, ensuring that the needs of each student are met and that students are empowered to take ownership of their learning journey. This change in mindset not only benefits students by providing them with a more engaging and supportive educational experience but also revitalizes teachers, who find renewed purpose and fulfillment in their roles as leaders of learning.

A truly transformative approach in education, however, requires more than just servant leadership. It necessitates a holistic strategy that integrates several key components: strong student-teacher relationships, an energetic and invigorating learning environment, student and teacher accountability, and a focus on cycling success. By viewing these elements as interconnected and interdependent, educators can create a classroom atmosphere that nurtures both academic achievement and personal growth.

Strong relationships between students and teachers form the bedrock of this holistic approach. When educators invest time and effort to understand their students' backgrounds, interests, strengths, and struggles, they lay the foundation for a trusting and supportive learning environment. Such relationships encourage open communication, mutual respect, and a genuine desire on the part of the student to succeed, knowing they have an ally in their teacher.

Complementing strong relationships is the necessity of crafting an energetic learning environment. An engaging classroom is one where creativity and excitement are palpable, stimulating students' natural curiosity. By incorporating diverse teaching strategies—such as project-based learning, collaborative activities, and the use of technology—teachers can cater to varied learning styles and interests, making education both enjoyable and effective.

Accountability is another crucial piece of this educational puzzle. In this context, it involves the establishment of clear expectations and responsibilities for both students and teachers. For students, accountability means taking charge of their learning and behavior. For teachers, it involves commitment to continuous professional development and adapting teaching practices to better serve their students. When all parties are held accountable, it fosters a culture of integrity, reliability, and continuous improvement.

The final—and perhaps most motivational—component is the cycle of success. Success encourages more success, and creating opportunities for students to experience small victories can build their confidence and enthusiasm for learning. When students see tangible results from their efforts, they are more likely to set higher goals and strive to achieve them. This positive reinforcement helps to maintain momentum and can lead to both improved academic outcomes and greater personal satisfaction.

In summary, the vision for transformative education is one where servant leadership, strong interpersonal connections, dynamic environments, accountability, and success are woven together to create a vibrant and effective teaching paradigm. As we navigate the complexities of modern education, embracing these principles can empower educators to inspire their students, meet their diverse needs, and prepare them to thrive in a rapidly changing world. This holistic approach not only transforms educational experiences but has the potential to transform lives, equipping students with the skills and confidence they need to succeed beyond the classroom walls. As educators, adopting this model can reignite our passion for nurturing young minds and shaping the future.

Chapter 6 - Defining Servant Leadership

Introduction: The Genesis of Servant Leadership

Servant leadership, a term first coined by Robert K. Greenleaf in his 1970 book "The Servant as Leader," reflects a profound shift from traditional leadership models. Greenleaf's foundational work introduced a paradigm where leaders primarily aim to serve others—a stark contrast to top-down, command-and-control approaches. The concept draws on timeless principles such as empathy, listening, stewardship, and a deep commitment to the growth and well-being of people, and it has implications that span various domains, including business, politics, and education.

The Origins and Principles of Servant Leadership

Robert K. Greenleaf, inspired by Hermann Hesse's novel Journey to the East, developed a paradigm-shifting perspective on leadership that prioritizes service over authority. (Greenleaf, 1964) He posited that authentic leadership does not stem from a desire for power, status, or control, but rather from an innate inclination to serve others. In Greenleaf's vision, the decision to lead is not an ambition driven by self-interest, but rather a response to the profound desire to uplift, empower, and support those within one's sphere of influence.

At the heart of Greenleaf's philosophical framework lies the unwavering belief that a servant leader prioritizes the well-being and development of those they guide. Unlike conventional leadership models that prioritize accumulating power or enforcing hierarchical structures, servant leadership is characterized by empathy, stewardship, and a steadfast commitment to the growth of others. A true servant leader recognizes their role as an enabler, removing obstacles, and fostering an environment conducive to flourishing.

In stark contrast to authoritarian or transactional leadership, where influence is maintained through rank and command, servant leadership inverts the traditional hierarchical structure. The leader serves the team, not the other way around. This paradigm-shift challenges conventional power dynamics and advocates for a relational and people-centered approach.

Greenleaf's profound insights were profoundly shaped by Hesse's novel Journey to the East, which chronicles the journey of a group of travelers guided by a humble servant named Leo. (Hess, 1956) Although Leo appears to be merely a facilitator, the group eventually comprehends that he was, in fact, their true leader—an unassuming individual who discreetly guided their mission and maintained the fabric of their collective success. When Leo mysteriously disappears, the journey descends into chaos. This parable deeply resonated with Greenleaf, who discerned a profound lesson on leadership: the most effective leaders are often those who serve without seeking recognition.

In contrast to traditional, hierarchical leadership models that often associate leadership with command, control, and personal advancement, Greenleaf's concept of servant leadership emphasizes support and nurturing. Servant leaders prioritize the growth and development of their followers, measuring success by fostering trust, collaboration, and a shared purpose. This approach is particularly effective in environments that require innovation, adaptability, and strong interpersonal relationships.

Greenleaf's philosophy has had a profound impact on various sectors, including business, education, and faith-based leadership. Organizations that adopt servant leadership often experience increased employee engagement, ethical decision-making, and long-term success. Today, this model is championed by leaders who prioritize inspiration over dominance, recognizing that the most enduring influence comes not from power, but from a heart dedicated to serving others. By redefining leadership as a calling to serve rather than a pursuit of status, Greenleaf's servant leadership model challenges leaders to lead with humility, compassion, and a deep commitment to the success of their teams.

Key Principles within Servant Leadership

Empathy: Empathy is one of the most essential qualities of a servant leader in the classroom, shaping the way educators connect with, support, and inspire their students. More than just acknowledging students' emotions, empathy requires a deep, intentional effort to understand their experiences, struggles, and aspirations. A servant-leader teacher creates an environment where students feel safe, valued, and motivated to learn because they know their teacher genuinely cares.

True empathy goes beyond simply listening to students' concerns—it involves actively observing, interpreting non-verbal cues, and responding with kindness and patience. Teachers with strong empathy recognize that each student comes from a unique background, facing personal challenges that may impact their ability to focus or succeed in the classroom. Whether a student struggles with academic difficulties, social pressures, or personal hardships, an empathetic teacher meets them with compassion rather than judgment.

By practicing empathy, educators build strong relationships that foster trust and open communication. When students feel heard and understood, they are more engaged, willing to take risks, and motivated to overcome obstacles. This sense of connection is particularly powerful for students who may feel overlooked or discouraged—a teacher's empathy can be the key to restoring their confidence and inspiring resilience.

Empathy also transforms classroom management and discipline. Instead of reacting harshly to mistakes or misbehavior, a servant-leader teacher seeks to understand the root cause and guide students toward growth. By offering constructive feedback, encouragement, and second chances, teachers not only shape academic success but also character development. Ultimately, empathy creates a classroom culture of kindness, respect, and belonging, where every student feels supported and empowered to reach their full potential.

Listening: Listening is a fundamental aspect of servant leadership in the classroom, shaping the way teachers engage with, support, and empower their students. A servant leader in education recognizes that communication is not just about speaking but also about truly hearing and understanding. Effective teachers prioritize active listening, making a conscious effort to absorb not only students' words but also their emotions, struggles, and unspoken concerns.

Active listening in the classroom involves more than just hearing responses to questions—it requires being present, observing body language, and creating an environment where students feel comfortable expressing themselves. Some students may not openly share their challenges, but a perceptive teacher notices subtle cues like hesitation, frustration, or disengagement, responding with care and attentiveness. By asking thoughtful questions, offering encouragement, and validating students' thoughts and feelings, a teacher demonstrates that each student's voice matters.

When students feel genuinely heard, they develop greater trust and confidence in their teacher, leading to increased engagement, motivation, and academic growth. A classroom where students feel safe to speak up—without fear of dismissal or criticism—fosters deeper learning, creativity, and collaboration. Listening also enables teachers to identify barriers to learning, whether they be academic struggles, social anxieties, or external challenges at home.

Moreover, listening enhances classroom management. A teacher who listens first rather than reacting impulsively can de-escalate conflicts, understand student behavior, and guide students with wisdom and patience. Ultimately, a servant leader in the classroom cultivates an atmosphere of respect and connection by prioritizing listening, ensuring that every student feels valued, supported, and empowered to succeed.

Healing: Healing is a profound aspect of servant leadership in the classroom, emphasizing a teacher's role in supporting students emotionally, mentally, and academically. A servant-leader educator understands that students bring more than just their academic abilities into the classroom—they bring their personal experiences, struggles, and challenges. By fostering a safe and encouraging environment, a teacher can help students overcome inner struggles, regain confidence, and develop resilience.

A healing-centered classroom begins with compassion and sensitivity. Some students may struggle with anxiety, low self-esteem, past academic failures, or difficult home environments. A servant-leader teacher is attuned to these challenges, offering patience, encouragement, and personalized support to help students thrive. This can be as simple as offering a kind word, providing extra help, or being a consistent, trustworthy presence in their lives.

Healing in education also means creating an environment where mistakes are seen as opportunities for growth, not sources of shame. Instead of punishing failure, a servant leader guides students toward reflection, problem-solving, and perseverance. This mindset fosters emotional and intellectual growth, teaching students to see challenges as stepping stones to success.

Furthermore, a teacher's encouragement can be life-changing, especially for students who feel overlooked or discouraged. A servant-leader educator helps students rediscover their potential, believe in themselves, and develop a positive self-image. Ultimately, a healing-oriented classroom is a place where students feel valued, supported, and empowered to grow—not just academically, but as whole individuals. A servant leader in education sees their role not just as an instructor, but as a mentor, encourager, and guide toward personal restoration and success.

Awareness: Awareness is a crucial principle of servant leadership in the classroom, requiring teachers to be mindful of both their own actions and the needs of their students. A servant-leader educator practices situational awareness, remaining attuned to classroom dynamics, student well-being, and potential challenges, while also cultivating self-awareness to ensure they lead with integrity and wisdom.

Situational awareness in the classroom means paying close attention to verbal and nonverbal cues, recognizing when students are struggling, disengaged, or in need of additional support. A teacher who is truly aware doesn't just follow a lesson plan rigidly but adapts to real-time needs, adjusting teaching strategies to create a more inclusive, engaging, and effective learning environment. This might involve modifying an assignment to accommodate different learning styles, sensing when a student needs encouragement, or diffusing tension in moments of conflict.

Self-awareness is just as important. A servant-leader teacher regularly reflects on their own biases, emotions, and teaching methods, ensuring they act ethically, respond thoughtfully, and remain open to growth. This involves being honest about mistakes, seeking feedback, and striving to improve. A self-aware educator understands that their words, tone, and actions have a profound impact on students and takes care to lead with fairness, humility, and respect.

Ultimately, awareness enhances a teacher's ability to make ethical decisions, build strong relationships, and create a responsive and compassionate classroom culture. A servant leader in education leads with insight and intention, ensuring that every student feels seen, heard, and supported in their journey toward growth and success.

Stewardship: Stewardship is a fundamental principle of servant leadership in the classroom, emphasizing a teacher's responsibility to manage resources wisely and nurture students to reach their fullest potential. A servant-leader educator understands that their role extends beyond delivering instruction—it involves caring for students' development, fostering a sense of responsibility, and creating an environment where both individuals and the classroom community thrive.

At its core, stewardship in education means being intentional about the well-being and growth of students. A servant-leader teacher does not simply aim for academic success but is invested in each student's personal and intellectual development. This involves encouraging curiosity, promoting critical thinking, and providing students with the tools they need to succeed both inside and outside the classroom. By guiding students rather than dictating to them, a steward-minded educator empowers students to take ownership of their learning, develop confidence, and cultivate responsibility for their own success.

Beyond nurturing individuals, stewardship also applies to managing classroom resources and creating a culture of respect. A servant-leader teacher ensures that class time, materials, and learning opportunities are used effectively, modeling integrity, sustainability, and responsibility. Additionally, stewardship involves fostering a classroom culture where students learn to respect one another, contribute to group success, and understand their role in a broader community.

Ultimately, stewardship in the classroom is about leading with care, intentionality, and a long-term vision for student success. A servant-leader teacher recognizes that their responsibility is not just to impart knowledge but to shape character, encourage responsibility, and prepare students to make meaningful contributions to the world.

Commitment to the Growth of People: A servant leader in the classroom is deeply committed to the growth and development of students—not just academically, but personally, socially, and emotionally. This principle of commitment to growth means that an educator sees each student as a unique individual with untapped potential and actively seeks to nurture that potential. A servant-leader teacher does not merely focus on delivering lessons but is invested in helping students develop confidence, resilience, and a lifelong love for learning.

This commitment manifests in mentorship, encouragement, and personalized support. A servant-leader teacher recognizes that students learn at different paces, come from diverse backgrounds, and face unique challenges. Instead of enforcing a one-size-fits-all approach, they adapt their teaching methods, provide individualized feedback, and offer resources to help students grow in ways that align with their strengths and needs. They celebrate progress over perfection, reinforcing that learning is a journey of continuous improvement.

Beyond academic instruction, a servant leader fosters students' emotional and ethical development, helping them grow into compassionate, responsible, and engaged members of their communities. They create a safe, nurturing environment where students feel empowered to take risks, ask questions, and explore new ideas.

A servant-leader educator also leads by example, demonstrating lifelong learning, humility, and self-improvement, inspiring students to develop these traits themselves. Ultimately, commitment to student growth transforms a classroom into a thriving, supportive community where students are not just taught but uplifted, encouraged, and prepared for success in all aspects of life.

From Traditional Leadership to Serving Others

Traditional leadership models often emphasize a top-down hierarchy, where power, authority, and decision-making primarily rest with those at the highest levels. In this model, leadership is often associated with control, efficiency, and meeting institutional goals, with employees, subordinates, or students positioned to serve the leader's directives. While this structure can ensure order and drive results, it frequently overlooks the personal and developmental needs of individuals, reducing leadership to a system of compliance rather than one of growth and empowerment.

In the classroom, a traditional leadership approach typically places the teacher in an authoritative role, where students are expected to listen, follow directions, and meet academic expectations. The teacher holds primary control, sets the agenda, and determines success based on performance metrics such as test scores and grades. While this structure maintains discipline and order, it can sometimes neglect student engagement, emotional well-being, and the cultivation of deeper learning.

Shifting to Servant Leadership in the Classroom

In contrast to traditional leadership, servant leadership inverts the pyramid by making leaders accountable to those they serve. In the classroom, this means that teachers are not just authority figures but facilitators, mentors, and supporters of student growth. A servant leader prioritizes students' needs, aspirations, and personal development, ensuring that learning is not just about academic performance but also about holistic growth—intellectual, emotional, and ethical.

Servant leadership in education fosters an inclusive, student-centered environment where learning is a collaborative journey rather than a rigidly structured process. Instead of positioning students as passive recipients of knowledge, servant-leader teachers empower students to take ownership of their learning, encouraging curiosity, creativity, and critical thinking.

Key Aspects of Servant Leadership in the Classroom

Prioritizing the Needs of Students: A servant-leader teacher understands that each student has unique strengths, challenges, and learning styles. Rather than enforcing a one-size-fits-all approach, they adapt their teaching methods, provide personalized support, and encourage students to explore their potential. By prioritizing the individual needs of students, a servant leader fosters a culture of inclusivity and belonging, where students feel safe to ask questions, take risks, and express their ideas.

For example, a traditional teacher may focus solely on covering curriculum objectives, while a servant-leader teacher considers how students are emotionally and intellectually engaging with the material. They ask questions like:

- *Are my students feeling supported in their learning process?*
- *Am I addressing different learning styles and needs?*
- *How can I help students build confidence and resilience?*

Building Meaningful Relationships and Trust: A core principle of servant leadership is the emphasis on relationships and trust. In the classroom, this means that teachers do not just dictate rules and expectations but instead create strong, positive connections with students. A servant-leader teacher listens actively, demonstrates empathy, and provides encouragement that goes beyond academic success.

Trust-building in education requires consistency, patience, and genuine investment in students' lives. Students who feel heard and valued are more likely to engage actively, contribute ideas, and develop intrinsic motivation. This shift from compliance-based learning to self-driven learning is one of the greatest benefits of servant leadership in education.

Encouraging Collaboration and Shared Success: Traditional leadership in the classroom often positions the teacher as the sole source of knowledge and decision-making, while students are expected to absorb information passively. Servant leadership, on the other hand, fosters a collaborative environment, where students are encouraged to engage in discussions, work together, and contribute their perspectives.

A servant-leader teacher facilitates learning rather than simply delivering content. They value student input, promote teamwork, and create opportunities for students to lead discussions and projects. This not only enhances engagement but also prepares students with real-world skills such as communication, problem-solving, and leadership.

Supporting Emotional and Personal Growth: Servant leadership in the classroom extends beyond academic instruction—it also prioritizes emotional well-being and character development. Many students face challenges such as self-doubt, anxiety, or external pressures, and a servant-leader teacher recognizes their role in guiding students through these struggles.

By creating a supportive classroom culture, teachers help students develop confidence, resilience, and a growth mindset. Mistakes and setbacks are not seen as failures, but as opportunities for learning and development. Encouragement, constructive feedback, and emotional support all contribute to a learning environment where students feel safe to take risks and strive for excellence.

Modeling Stewardship and Responsibility: A servant leader in the classroom models stewardship, teaching students the importance of responsibility, respect, and care for their community. By demonstrating ethical leadership, accountability, and service, a teacher inspires students to adopt these values in their own lives.

For example, a servant-leader teacher might encourage students to mentor their peers, take initiative in group projects, or contribute to classroom discussions in meaningful ways. They foster an understanding that success is not just about individual achievement but about uplifting others and working toward a common goal.

The Impact of Servant Leadership in the Classroom

By shifting from traditional leadership to serving students first, educators create classrooms that are more engaging, inclusive, and empowering. Research suggests that servant leadership leads to higher levels of student motivation, improved classroom relationships, and better long-term academic and personal success. (Kuhnert, 2016)

My experience is that students who learn under servant-leader teachers are more likely to:

- Take ownership of their learning
- Develop stronger communication and problem-solving skills
- Cultivate self-confidence and resilience
- Foster respect and empathy for others

Moreover, when teachers lead with a mindset of service, they help shape not only knowledgeable students but also compassionate, thoughtful individuals who will carry these values into their future careers and communities.

Moving from traditional leadership to servant leadership in the classroom is a transformational shift that prioritizes people over processes, relationships over authority, and long-term growth over short-term results. While traditional models may focus on instructional efficiency, servant leadership ensures that every student is seen, heard, and supported in their learning journey.

By adopting a leadership approach centered on service, teachers become not just instructors, but mentors, role models, and catalysts for lifelong growth. In doing so, they create an educational experience that is meaningful, empowering, and impactful, shaping students who are not only academically strong but also equipped with the skills and mindset to lead, serve, and thrive in the world beyond the classroom.

Conclusion: A Call for Transformative Educational Leadership

Implementing servant leadership in the classroom creates lasting, positive impacts on both students and teachers. Students mentored under servant-leader principles often demonstrate improved academic performance, enhanced critical thinking skills, and increased emotional intelligence. They learn the value of serving others, which resonates well into adulthood, helping them to become compassionate and effective leaders.

For educators, embodying the servant-leader ethos means developing deeper personal connections with students and colleagues, cultivating a more supportive and fulfilling work environment. This approach is sustainably enriching, combating burnout, and inspiring passion for teaching.

Defining servant leadership by its foundational principles offers a blueprint for transformative leadership across all educational levels. Underpinning this philosophy with empathy, listening, stewardship, and a commitment to growth, educators can profoundly influence systemic change in how teaching and learning unfold.

By embracing servant leadership, educators now stand at the frontier of reshaping educational landscapes to be more inclusive and responsive—emphasizing collaboration over competition and community over hierarchy. The cultivation of environments where empathy and partnership are mainstays is fundamental to thriving academic ecosystems dedicated to lifelong learning.

Ultimately, by committing to serve, educate, and inspire, we leverage untapped human potential, allowing servant leadership to not just direct our schools, but indelibly enrich our wider society as well. It's a vision that not only leads—it serves by empowering others to foster shared visions of success.

Reflection and Action Step

How do I currently demonstrate empathy toward my students, and in what ways can I deepen my understanding of their individual experiences and challenges?

In what ways do I actively listen to my students—both their words and their unspoken cues—and how can I improve my ability to make every student feel truly heard

How do I foster a classroom environment where students feel safe to express their struggles and seek support, and what steps can I take to further promote healing and resilience?

What practices do I use to remain aware of both my students' needs and my own biases or habits as an educator, and how can I become more responsive and self-aware in my teaching?

In what ways do I model stewardship and a commitment to student growth, and how can I better empower students to take ownership of their own learning and development?

Action Step

Choose one core principle of servant leadership (empathy, listening, healing, awareness, stewardship, or commitment to growth) and intentionally focus on strengthening it in your classroom this week?

Chapter 7 - Building Strong Relationships with Students

Introduction: The Foundation of Trust in Education

Education is far more than the simple transmission of knowledge; it is a deeply human endeavor that thrives on relationships. At the heart of every meaningful educational experience lies the bond between teachers and their students. This relationship is not merely a byproduct of the classroom setting but rather a crucial determinant of student success and personal growth. A trusting and supportive learning environment emerges when teachers take the time to develop meaningful connections with their students, demonstrating genuine care, respect, and investment in their well-being. These relationships form the bedrock upon which students feel valued, understood, and motivated to reach their full potential.

The significance of fostering trust in education cannot be overstated. Research consistently shows that students who feel connected to their teachers exhibit higher levels of engagement, improved academic performance, and enhanced emotional well-being. (Pianta, Hamre, & Allen, 2012) Beyond academics, a strong teacher-student relationship equips learners with the confidence and resilience necessary to navigate life's challenges. When students perceive their teachers as approachable, understanding, and invested in their success, they are more likely to participate actively, seek help when needed, and develop a positive attitude toward learning.

However, building these vital connections requires intentional effort and an understanding of the diverse backgrounds, experiences, and learning styles that students bring to the classroom. Every student enters the learning environment with unique perspectives shaped by their cultural, socioeconomic, and personal histories. Acknowledging and appreciating this diversity is essential for creating an inclusive classroom where every student feels seen, heard, and respected. When teachers take the time to understand their students' backgrounds and challenges, they demonstrate empathy and build rapport, fostering a culture of mutual respect and collaboration.

To cultivate strong relationships with students, educators must employ a variety of strategies that go beyond traditional instructional methods. One fundamental approach is active listening. By truly hearing students' concerns, aspirations, and struggles, teachers can create an open and supportive dialogue that encourages trust. Another key practice is personalized engagement, where teachers tailor their interactions and teaching methods to meet the needs of individual students. Simple gestures such as greeting students by name, acknowledging their achievements, and showing interest in their lives outside the classroom can significantly enhance the teacher-student bond.

Moreover, the establishment of a positive classroom culture plays a crucial role in strengthening these relationships. Teachers who foster a sense of community, encourage collaboration, and model respect create an environment where students feel safe to express themselves and take academic risks. By setting clear expectations and maintaining consistency in their interactions, educators provide a sense of stability and reliability that further reinforces trust.

Beyond the immediate classroom setting, the impact of strong teacher-student relationships extends into students' long-term development. A teacher who believes in their students' abilities and encourages them to persevere can inspire lifelong confidence and a love for learning. Many successful individuals attribute their achievements to a teacher who took the time to connect with them and inspire their growth. I hold cherished memories of my previous educators, including Lois Killingsworth (5th grade teacher), Kerry Moore (speech and theater teacher), and Anthony Gibson (band director). Today, I have integrated many of their positive qualities into my own teaching style. These meaningful connections leave a lasting imprint, shaping students' attitudes toward education and their future aspirations.

In conclusion, the foundation of trust in education is built upon the relationships teachers cultivate with their students. By prioritizing connection, empathy, and understanding, educators create a learning environment where students feel supported and motivated to succeed. This chapter delves into the importance of personal connections in education, explores methods for appreciating student diversity, and provides practical strategies for fostering strong teacher-student relationships. Ultimately, a culture of trust and support within the classroom not only enhances academic outcomes but also nurtures students' overall well-being and lifelong success.

The Importance of Personal Connections with Students

A fundamental aspect of effective teaching is the ability to connect with students beyond the confines of academic content. When students perceive that teachers genuinely care about them as individuals, they are more likely to engage, participate, and invest their time and effort in learning. Establishing a personal connection with students goes beyond simply knowing their names; it involves understanding their backgrounds, interests, and unique learning needs. Every year, I work diligently to get to know my students personally to create a learning space that prioritizes safety, openness, and mutual respect, where the uniqueness of every student is acknowledged and celebrated.

Personal connections contribute to a positive learning atmosphere where mistakes are seen as opportunities for growth rather than failures. Students tend to thrive academically and emotionally in environments where they feel confident enough to express their thoughts and concerns without fear of judgment or retribution. Trusting relationships encourage students to take intellectual risks, embrace challenges, and ultimately, achieve higher levels of academic performance. When students believe that their teachers are invested in their success, they are more likely to push themselves beyond their comfort zones, actively participate in discussions, and take initiative in their own learning journeys. I frequently assert that I do not believe I am a superior educator compared to many of my colleagues. Nevertheless, my success can be attributed to the positive relationships I have cultivated with my students. These positive relationships have resulted in most of my students exerting greater effort for me than they did for their previous teachers.

Furthermore, developing personal connections aids in the recognition of each student's strengths and areas needing improvement, paving the way for tailored educational experiences that cater to individual needs. Teachers who know their students well are more effective in differentiating instruction to accommodate diverse learning styles and capabilities, leading to an inclusive classroom. Understanding students' unique challenges and aspirations allows educators to design lesson plans that resonate with their interests and make learning more engaging and meaningful. This differentiation ensures that all students receive the support they need to succeed, regardless of their starting points.

Beyond academic performance, personal connections also play a vital role in students' emotional and social development. Many students face challenges outside the classroom that can impact their ability to focus and learn effectively. By establishing strong relationships, teachers can identify signs of distress, offer guidance, and connect students with the necessary resources and support systems. A teacher who genuinely listens and provides encouragement can make a significant difference in a student's self-esteem, resilience, and overall well-being.

One of the most effective ways to build personal connections is through active and empathetic listening. When teachers take the time to listen attentively to their students' concerns, interests, and aspirations, they create a foundation of trust and respect. Simple gestures, such as remembering important details about a student's life, acknowledging their achievements, and checking in on their well-being, can go a long way in fostering meaningful relationships.

Another essential strategy is creating a classroom culture that values collaboration and mutual support. Encouraging peer interactions, group discussions, and team projects allows students to feel a sense of belonging and shared purpose. In my flexible-seating classroom, students have the option to sit in various configurations, including couches, chairs, dining room tables, and high-top tables. While students generally have freedom to choose their seating, I occasionally assign specific students to sit together at designated tables or area. This approach not only fosters peer interaction and a sense of belonging among students but also enables me to effectively utilize their unique strengths. For instance, if a student is a verbal learner, it is crucial for them to engage in discussions to grasp a particular topic. By placing this student next to a struggling student, they can provide verbal guidance and support, facilitating the learning process for their seat partner. A supportive classroom environment where students uplift and inspire one another fosters a positive learning experience and strengthens the bonds between teachers and students alike.

Additionally, integrating student interests into the curriculum enhances engagement and strengthens relationships. When students see that their passions and hobbies are reflected in their lessons, they become more motivated and invested in their learning. One seemingly insignificant aspect of my teaching practice involves incorporating students' names into digital or on-line platform assignments. By utilizing students' strengths or interests as the basis for questions, I aim to foster a sense of engagement and excitement among them. Notably, students consistently express enthusiasm when they encounter their names on Wayground (formerly Quizizz) or Gimkit problems. Teachers can achieve this by incorporating relevant examples, allowing students to choose project topics that resonate with them, and integrating hands-on activities that connect classroom content to real-world experiences.

Building connections also involves modeling the values of empathy, kindness, and respect. When educators demonstrate genuine care for their students and treat them with dignity, students, in turn, learn to model these behaviors in their interactions with peers and teachers. By fostering a culture of respect and appreciation, educators create an environment where students feel safe, valued, and empowered to express themselves authentically. This principle is demonstrated when the opposite occurs. I am not perfect; I am a human being with flaws. On those rare occasions when I have not treated my students with the dignity they deserve, I witness the profound emotional distress and significant withdrawal they experience towards me. A well-known adage suggests that it takes ten positive words or actions to compensate for a single negative. My personal experience indicates that it can take several days to mend the damage caused by a single "off" day.

Furthermore, strong teacher-student relationships have lasting effects beyond the classroom. Many students carry the impact of a supportive teacher throughout their lives, using the encouragement and mentorship they received as a source of motivation in their future endeavors. Some even return years later to express gratitude for the role their teachers played in shaping their aspirations and achievements. The ripple effect of meaningful connections in education extends far beyond the school years, influencing students' confidence, career paths, and personal development.

The importance of personal connections with students cannot be overstated. These relationships create a learning environment where students feel valued, supported, and motivated to succeed. By fostering trust, recognizing individual strengths, and implementing inclusive teaching strategies, educators can create a classroom atmosphere that encourages academic growth, emotional well-being, and lifelong learning. Teaching is not just about delivering content; it is about inspiring and uplifting students, empowering them to believe in their potential, and equipping them with the confidence and skills to navigate the world beyond the classroom.

Techniques for Understanding Students' Backgrounds

The first step in building strong relationships with students involves understanding their unique personal, emotional, and educational backgrounds. Teachers must practice active listening and empathy to discover what influences students outside the classroom. An awareness of familial, cultural, and socioeconomic factors provides context, influencing how students perceive authority and approach their studies.

To achieve this understanding, educators can employ various techniques:

Get to Know Your Students Personally: Building personal connections with students is an essential aspect of creating a supportive and effective learning environment. Teachers can begin by incorporating simple ice-breaking activities at the start of the school year, allowing students to introduce themselves and share their personal interests, hobbies, and aspirations. These activities help students feel more comfortable while offering teachers valuable insights into each student's personality, strengths, and preferences. Beyond initial introductions, teachers should continue fostering relationships throughout the year by engaging in informal conversations, acknowledging students' achievements, and demonstrating genuine interest in their lives outside of the classroom.

Establishing a connection requires intentionality and consistency. One way to deepen relationships is by integrating students' interests into lesson plans. For instance, if a student is passionate about music, a teacher can incorporate song lyrics into language lessons or discuss the mathematical patterns in music. Recognizing students' hobbies and incorporating them into classroom discussions not only validates their identities but also makes learning more engaging and meaningful.

Another effective strategy is to create structured moments for personal sharing. Setting aside time for "Student Spotlight" sessions, where students voluntarily share something about themselves, can encourage openness and create an inclusive atmosphere. One of the most positive initiatives implemented at Jacksboro Middle School is the Spotlighting program, which recognizes students for their accomplishments. Students are publicly acknowledged on the school's Facebook page. It is gratifying to observe positive comments in the feed regarding these students. This program has demonstrated significant value in fostering a culture of achievement and inspiring future success. Additionally, maintaining a class tradition, such as

"Friday Reflections," where students talk about their week, their challenges, and their successes, fosters a sense of community and trust.

Teachers should also be observant of students' non-verbal cues and emotional states. A student who is unusually quiet or withdrawn may be experiencing personal challenges. By checking in with students individually and offering a supportive ear, teachers demonstrate their commitment to student well-being beyond academics. This can be as simple as asking, "How was your weekend?" or "Is everything okay?" Small but meaningful interactions can build rapport and encourage students to confide in their teachers when needed.

Furthermore, teachers can encourage collaborative activities that promote peer interaction and strengthen classroom relationships. Group projects, partner activities, and peer mentoring opportunities enable students to connect with one another while allowing teachers to observe their social dynamics and preferences. Understanding students within their social contexts provides deeper insight into how they interact, communicate, and learn best.

Building relationships does not stop in the classroom. Participating in student events, such as sporting competitions, musical performances, and community gatherings, demonstrates to students that their educators recognize their worth beyond academic achievements. I actively participate in most home games for our sports teams and concerts for our band. Occasionally, I extend my support by attending away cross-country meets. Furthermore, collaborating with my teaching partner, Caroline Vaughn, we diligently capture and display numerous photographs of our students at these events throughout the hallways. Students invariably glance at these photographs, and it is gratifying to observe their smiles and positive remarks. Additionally, I mail birthday cards to every student with a personalized note. I buy a box of birthday cards for approximately $30 on Amazon and utilize them throughout the academic year. While this endeavor requires effort, time, and postage, students greatly appreciate receiving these cards in the mail. Many students express their gratitude with a hug and a heartfelt thank-you after receiving their cards. These efforts reinforce trust, mutual respect, and a positive learning atmosphere, making students feel supported and understood.

Getting to know students personally requires ongoing effort, but it is a fundamental aspect of effective teaching. By engaging in meaningful conversations, integrating student interests into lessons, facilitating personal sharing, and demonstrating empathy, teachers can build authentic connections that enhance both academic success and personal development. When students feel genuinely valued, they are more likely to be motivated, engaged, and open to learning experiences that shape their future.

Conduct Student Surveys: Distributing questionnaires can serve as a structured approach to gather information about students' learning goals, habits, and preferences. This data guides pedagogical strategies and aids in forming personal connections based on an appreciation of students' distinct perspectives.

Surveys can be customized to include a wide range of topics, from academic interests to personal learning challenges. Questions can explore preferred learning styles, extracurricular activities, classroom expectations, and even students' feelings about different subjects. The flexibility of surveys allows educators to gain a more comprehensive understanding of their students while offering an avenue for students to express themselves honestly.

Administering surveys at different points in the academic year ensures that teachers remain attuned to changes in students' attitudes, needs, and goals. An initial survey at the beginning of the school year helps set the foundation for individualized instruction, while periodic check-ins can highlight shifts in motivation, engagement, or areas where students require additional support. Exit surveys at the end of the year also provide valuable feedback for improving future teaching methods. To maximize effectiveness, teachers should create both structured and open-ended survey questions. Multiple-choice or rating-scale questions can help identify patterns and trends, while open-ended responses offer deeper insights into students' thoughts, challenges, and aspirations. Encouraging students to share their personal and academic goals allows teachers to provide relevant guidance and adapt their instructional approaches accordingly. Every year, my students fill out a report card for me. They do this through a survey that's shared in Google Classroom. In addition to rating me on a scale from 1 to 5 (1 being terrible and 5 being amazing), there are also open-ended questions that ask for suggestions on how I can improve as a teacher. Overall, the students are very honest and straightforward. I read every single submission and make changes to my teaching based on many of these suggestions.

Beyond traditional surveys, technology can be leveraged to make the process more engaging. Online survey tools, interactive polls, or anonymous response platforms give students the freedom to express themselves without hesitation. Teachers can also gamify the process by incorporating surveys into classroom activities, making them feel less like assessments and more like opportunities for self-expression.

Importantly, surveys should not be a one-time event but rather a continuous method for understanding students. Following up on survey responses, acknowledging concerns, and adjusting teaching strategies based on student feedback reinforces that their opinions are valued. When students see that their input directly influences their learning experience, they develop a stronger sense of ownership over their education. Honestly, I don't do this. I'm not organized enough to send out surveys throughout the year. However, I do ask for feedback often from my students throughout the year.

Student surveys are a powerful tool for understanding learners on a deeper level. By systematically gathering information about student needs, preferences, and backgrounds, teachers can create a more personalized and supportive educational experience. Integrating surveys into classroom practices fosters engagement, strengthens relationships, and ensures that teaching methods remain responsive to the evolving needs of students.

Hold One-on-One Meetings: Scheduling regular, informal discussions with students can be invaluable in deepening understanding. These meetings provide opportunities for students to voice concerns and aspirations directly, build rapport, and receive undivided attention from teachers.

One-on-one meetings allow educators to gain insight into students' personal challenges, academic goals, and overall well-being. These conversations foster trust, enabling students to feel comfortable discussing any obstacles they may be facing in their education or personal lives. Teachers can schedule short but frequent check-ins to keep communication open, ensuring that students feel seen and heard throughout the academic year.

These meetings can also help teachers tailor instruction to better meet individual student needs. Whether it's identifying a struggling student who requires additional support or recognizing a student's unique talents and interests, personalized interactions make a significant difference in academic success. When students feel their voices matter, they are more likely to be engaged and motivated in their learning.

Implementing an open-door policy further reinforces accessibility and trust. Encouraging students to approach teachers whenever they need assistance or simply to talk fosters an environment of mutual respect and support. Additionally, providing multiple formats for meetings—such as in-person discussions, virtual check-ins, or written reflections—ensures that all students feel comfortable expressing themselves.

Overall, one-on-one meetings are a powerful tool for strengthening teacher-student relationships. They create space for meaningful dialogue, enhance personalized learning, and contribute to a supportive educational experience. By prioritizing regular check-ins, teachers can build lasting connections that positively impact students' academic and personal growth.

Strategies to Strengthen Student-Teacher Relationships

With a foundational understanding of students' backgrounds, teachers can implement a range of strategies to strengthen their relationships with students. Building strong student-teacher relationships requires intentional efforts to create trust, foster engagement, and promote a positive learning environment. Strengthening these relationships enhances student motivation, increases classroom participation, and supports academic and personal growth. A teacher's ability to connect with students on a meaningful level goes beyond academics—it instills confidence, fosters resilience, and promotes a culture of respect and empathy. Implementing specific approaches in daily teaching practices can significantly impact the quality of interactions between students and educators.

Regular feedback plays a vital role in student development. Providing timely, constructive, and personalized feedback helps students recognize their strengths and understand areas for improvement. Feedback should go beyond grades, offering detailed suggestions and encouragement. Acknowledging student effort fosters a growth mindset, reinforcing the idea that learning is a continuous process. Feedback should be framed in a way that motivates students rather than discouraging them. Engaging in one-on-one discussions about progress and setting achievable goals empowers students to take ownership of their learning. When students feel that their work is valued and appreciated, they become more invested in their education.

Open communication fosters transparency and trust between students and teachers. Creating an environment where students feel comfortable expressing their thoughts, asking questions, and sharing concerns helps cultivate meaningful connections. Encouraging students to provide feedback on teaching methods, classroom activities, and their overall learning experiences demonstrates that their opinions matter. It's awesome when students share their thoughts on how we teach and what they learn. I always ask during lessons if I'm explaining things clearly. Sometimes, they say I'm doing a great job, but other times, they'll say I lost them somewhere. That's when I know I need to go back and explain things again. Teachers who implement an open-door policy reinforce accessibility and support, allowing students to seek guidance, share challenges, or celebrate achievements. Active listening is crucial in open communication—teachers should practice patience and show genuine interest in what students have to say. By fostering dialogue, teachers build an atmosphere of mutual respect and understanding, which enhances the overall classroom dynamic.

Establishing a supportive classroom environment is essential for student success. A positive classroom culture encourages inclusivity, respect, and collaboration. Setting clear expectations for behavior and interaction promotes a safe and welcoming space where students feel valued. Social-emotional learning principles can be incorporated to teach students how to navigate interpersonal relationships, manage emotions, and develop empathy. Facilitating group work, peer discussions, and team-based projects strengthens peer relationships and fosters a sense of community. When students feel safe and respected in their classroom, they are more likely to engage and participate actively in their learning.

Providing personalized support enhances student confidence and academic success. Recognizing that each student has unique learning needs allows teachers to adapt their instructional approaches accordingly. Tailoring study materials, modifying assignments, and offering additional resources demonstrate a commitment to individualized learning. Differentiated instruction helps accommodate diverse learning styles and abilities, ensuring that each student receives the support they need to thrive. Personal mentorship opportunities, such as guiding students in extracurricular activities or career planning, further strengthen the student-teacher bond. When students receive encouragement tailored to their needs, they feel seen and supported in their educational journey.

Empowering students with choices fosters autonomy and engagement. Allowing students to have a say in their learning process increases motivation and investment in their education. Teachers can provide opportunities for students to select project topics, participate in decision-making about class rules, or contribute ideas for classroom discussions. Offering choices in assessments, such as written assignments, presentations, or creative projects, accommodates different learning preferences and strengths. When students feel that they have control over aspects of their learning, they become more responsible and proactive in their academic pursuits. This sense of ownership leads to higher levels of engagement and a stronger connection between students and their teachers.

Celebrating student achievements, both big and small, contributes to a positive and encouraging classroom atmosphere. Recognizing students for their efforts, progress, and accomplishments boosts self-esteem and motivation. Simple gestures such as verbal praise, written notes of encouragement, or public recognition in class help students feel valued. Teachers can implement reward systems, certificates, or classroom shout-outs to acknowledge student successes. Even minor improvements or acts of kindness should be celebrated, reinforcing the importance of perseverance and personal growth. When students feel appreciated and recognized, they develop a stronger sense of belonging in the classroom community.

Modeling and encouraging empathy within the classroom promote a culture of understanding and support. Teachers serve as role models, and their behavior significantly impacts classroom interactions. Demonstrating kindness, patience, and active listening sets a precedent for students to follow. Encouraging students to practice empathy in their peer interactions strengthens social connections and fosters an inclusive classroom environment. Activities such as peer mentoring, group discussions on real-world issues, and reflective exercises help students develop emotional intelligence. When empathy is a core classroom value, students learn to support one another, creating a harmonious and cooperative learning environment.

Consistency and reliability in teacher-student interactions reinforce trust and security. Being dependable, maintaining fairness, and following through on commitments show students that they can rely on their teachers. Establishing routines and clear expectations provides stability, reducing anxiety and uncertainty. A consistent approach to discipline, encouragement, and classroom management ensures that all students feel treated with fairness and respect. When students trust that their teachers are committed to their well-being, they are more likely to engage in learning and seek help when needed.

Encouraging student self-expression strengthens student-teacher relationships by giving students a voice in their education. Providing platforms for students to share their thoughts, ideas, and personal experiences creates a dynamic and engaging learning environment. Incorporating journaling, classroom discussions, storytelling, and student-led presentations allows students to express themselves freely. Teachers who actively listen and respond to student perspectives build stronger relationships based on mutual respect and understanding. Recognizing students' identities and valuing their contributions reinforce their sense of self-worth and agency in their education.

Engaging with students outside the classroom further strengthens bonds and demonstrates genuine care. Attending school events, extracurricular activities, and student performances shows support beyond academics. Participating in informal interactions, such as lunch discussions or school-wide initiatives, allows teachers to connect with students in a relaxed setting. When students see that their teachers take an interest in their lives beyond the curriculum, they feel a greater sense of connection and belonging.

In conclusion, building strong student-teacher relationships requires intentional effort and ongoing commitment. Implementing strategies such as open communication, personalized support, student empowerment, and consistent encouragement fosters a positive and engaging learning environment. Teachers who prioritize connection, empathy, and student well-being create classrooms where students feel valued, motivated, and inspired. When students experience a genuine and supportive relationship with their teachers, they develop the confidence, resilience, and enthusiasm needed to thrive academically and personally. Strengthening these relationships not only enhances academic outcomes but also shapes students into lifelong learners and empowered individuals.

Conclusion: The Path to Meaningful Educational Experiences

Building strong relationships with students is more than a pedagogical strategy; it is a commitment to fostering future generations. Understanding the personal nuances of each student enriches the educational experience by establishing environments where learning transcends beyond academics, developing emotionally intelligent, resilient, and thoughtful citizens.

By focusing on meaningful connections, teachers pave the way for better cognitive, emotional, and social outcomes for their students. Techniques such as understanding students' backgrounds and fostering empathy, combined with strategies like regular feedback, open communication, and personalized support, are vital components to developing and sustaining strong student-teacher relationships. Ultimately, the cultivation of these relationships shapes students who are prepared not merely to excel in school, but to contribute meaningfully to society—a testament to any educator's greatest mission.

Reflection and Action Step

How do I currently motivate students who are discouraged or lack confidence in my subject area, and what new strategies can I try to help them see their potential for growth?

In what ways can I make my lessons more engaging for students who are not naturally interested in the material?

What specific steps can I take to help students set and achieve realistic learning goals in my classroom?

How do I recognize and celebrate student effort and progress, not just final achievement?

How do you reinforce the value of persistence and improvement? Think about incorporating more frequent feedback, peer recognition, or classroom celebrations that focus on effort as much as outcome.

What strategies can I use to help students overcome negative beliefs about their abilities, such as "I'm just not a math person"?

Action Step

At the start of a new unit, have each student set a personal learning goal related to the subject (e.g., mastering a specific concept or improving a test score). Frame the learning process as a journey toward achieving something meaningful to them. Regularly remind students that, like athletes coached to push beyond their comfort zones, they are working toward their own aspirations—even when the work feels challenging. Use encouraging, coaching-style language to reinforce that overcoming difficulties is part of reaching their goals.

Chapter 8 - Creating a Fun, Energetic Learning Environment

Introduction: The Key to Effective Teaching and Learning

Learning should never feel like a chore—it should be an adventure! Education isn't just about memorizing facts or passing tests; it's about sparking curiosity, encouraging creativity, and making discovery exciting. When students are engaged, laughing, and genuinely enjoying the learning process, they absorb information more easily and develop a love for learning that sticks with them for life. That's why creating a fun, high-energy classroom is so important. It transforms education from something students *have* to do into something they *want* to do.

Think about it—when students walk into a classroom filled with energy, movement, and interactive activities, they're instantly more engaged. Compare that to a dull, lecture-heavy environment where they're just sitting and listening. Which one do you think will make a bigger impact? A classroom that feels alive with games, challenges, and hands-on experiences fosters motivation, teamwork, and deeper understanding. It gives students the freedom to experiment, ask questions, and truly connect with the material in ways that go beyond rote memorization.

But here's the trick: balancing that energy with structure. Too much chaos can lead to distraction, and too much structure can make learning feel rigid and boring. The sweet spot lies in blending creativity with organization—giving students room to explore while still guiding them toward meaningful learning outcomes.

In this chapter, I'll share some of my favorite techniques for making learning exciting, from interactive games to creative teaching styles that keep students on their toes. Whether it's turning a history lesson into an escape room, using friendly competitions to review material, or incorporating movement into math exercises, these methods help keep students engaged and motivated. I'll also discuss how to adapt these strategies to different subjects and learning styles so that every student—whether they thrive in hands-on activities or prefer a structured approach—can benefit.

At the end of the day, learning should be something kids look forward to, not something they endure. A lively, engaging classroom isn't just more fun—it's more effective. Let's dive into some strategies that will make learning an unforgettable experience!

The Power of a Positive and Dynamic Classroom Environment

A classroom filled with energy, encouragement, and positivity can transform the way students learn. When students walk into a space that feels welcoming and alive, they're more likely to engage, participate, and tackle challenges with confidence. A dynamic learning environment creates a sense of belonging where students feel safe expressing their thoughts and ideas, knowing they won't be judged for making mistakes. This sense of security helps build self-confidence, reduces anxiety, and fosters a love for learning that extends far beyond the classroom.

Research shows that students thrive in engaging and stimulating classrooms. (Shirley & Hargreaves, 1995) When lessons are interactive, students don't just passively absorb information—they actively connect with it. A high-energy environment encourages curiosity and intrinsic motivation, which is key to long-term academic success. When students enjoy learning, they develop a natural desire to explore, think critically, and seek out knowledge on their own.

But the benefits of a positive classroom go beyond academics. When students work together in a dynamic setting, they develop essential life skills like teamwork, communication, and adaptability. Group projects, hands-on activities, and class discussions teach students how to collaborate, listen, and respect different perspectives. These skills are not only vital for school success but also for future careers and everyday interactions.

Moreover, a lively classroom promotes creativity and problem-solving. When students are encouraged to think outside the box, take risks, and experiment with new ideas, they become more innovative thinkers. A rigid, overly structured environment can stifle creativity, but a balanced approach—where structure meets spontaneity—creates a space where students feel empowered to learn in ways that work best for them.

Teachers play a huge role in setting the tone. Enthusiasm is contagious! If an educator brings passion and energy into their teaching, students will feed off that excitement. By fostering a positive and engaging classroom, teachers don't just help students succeed academically—they inspire them to become lifelong learners. A dynamic learning space makes education not just something students have to do, but something they truly want to be a part of.

Examples of Activities and Teaching Styles to Boost Energy and Engagement

Creating an engaging and energetic classroom requires creativity, innovation, and a mix of teaching styles that cater to different learning needs. Below are some dynamic strategies that successful educators use to keep students motivated and excited about learning:

Interactive Games and Challenges: Interactive games and challenges are a cornerstone of my classroom, serving not only to reinforce key math concepts but also to spark excitement and engagement. By integrating platforms like Kahoot!, Gimkit, Blookit, and Wayground (formerly Quizizz), I transform standard reviews into fast-paced, competitive sessions that students actually look forward to. These game-based approaches make learning more dynamic; students participate eagerly, absorb material more deeply, and often surprise themselves with how much they enjoy the process.

Beyond digital platforms, I make learning active through a variety of hands-on games. My room features a nerf basketball goal, which becomes the centerpiece for many review sessions. During these activities, I split students into teams: after successfully solving a math problem on the board, students earn a chance to shoot a basket. This blend of academic challenge and physical movement keeps students alert and invigorated—suddenly, practicing equations or polynomials is associated with laughter and friendly rivalry.

To further enhance engagement, I use items like nerf guns, sucker balls, and a golf mat for station-based reviews. Here, students rotate between activities, and each accurate solution gives them the chance to hit a target or sink a putt. Not only do these games foster critical thinking and teamwork, but they also help even the most reserved students come out of their shells, especially when cheered on by their classmates.

Adding an extra layer of motivation, I introduce "Carpenter Cash"—our classroom economic currency. Whenever students participate in these games, they have opportunities to earn Carpenter Cash by demonstrating skill, teamwork, or a positive attitude. This cash can be used to purchase snacks, extra credit points, computer free time, homework passes, and other small privileges. The system turns participation into a real-life reward scenario, fueling friendly competition and encouraging everyone to get involved.

By weaving these interactive games with the Carpenter Cash incentive, I create an environment where learning is lively, collaborative, and highly motivating. Students leave class not only with sharper math skills but also with a strong sense of accomplishment and the lasting memory that learning can—and should—be both rewarding and a lot of fun.

Hands-on Learning: Hands-on learning is a cornerstone of my teaching philosophy, especially in math, where abstract ideas can sometimes feel distant or confusing to students. I firmly believe that students learn best when they are actively involved—seeing, touching, doing—rather than just passively listening to a lesson. Transforming math concepts into tangible, interactive activities not only boost engagement but also makes those concepts stick, fostering deeper understanding and longer-lasting retention.

In my math classroom, I routinely incorporate manipulatives and hands-on projects to help students bridge the gap between theory and practice. When we study fractions, for instance, I bring out fraction tiles and let students physically build and compare different values. They might piece together tiles to represent equations like or solve problems by rearranging shapes. This physical interaction allows students to move beyond memorization—they actually see and feel how fractions combine or break apart, making those relationships much clearer.

Geometric concepts lend themselves particularly well to hands-on exploration. When we cover area and perimeter, I give students grid paper, scissors, and colored tiles to create shapes, calculate measurements, and even compose their own "mini-cities" using a set number of square units. For three-dimensional concepts like volume, we might use connecting cubes to build different rectangular prisms, so students can count layers and truly understand how volume accumulates within an object.

Sometimes I set up classroom engineering challenges, like constructing bridges from straws or toothpicks and testing their strength with weights or small classroom objects. These activities naturally spark curiosity, creative problem-solving, and collaboration, as students experiment, hypothesize, and adjust their designs. Their pride in seeing a successful structure or solution is profound, and the connections to underlying math concepts become much stronger.

Recently, I adapted a lesson using the classroom nerf basketball goal: students calculated shooting angles and probabilities, then collected data on their shots to create graphs and analyze outcomes. Not only was engagement sky-high, but students also walked away with a practical understanding of statistics and experimental probability that felt truly relevant.

By transforming math into a hands-on experience, I've seen students who once struggled with abstract concepts become more confident and eager to participate. Learning becomes an adventure, and my classroom turns into a space where discovery and exploration drive real growth.

Art and Music Integration: Integrating art and music into academics is a dynamic way to enhance understanding and make the learning experience much more engaging for students. By encouraging creative expression through drawing, painting, singing, or songwriting, students are able to connect with material on a deeper, more personal level. When learners are allowed to communicate what they know in diverse ways, lessons become memorable, stimulating multiple senses and reinforcing comprehension.

In my math classroom, I often encourage students to create visual representations of abstract concepts. For example, they might design colorful posters that illustrate the steps of solving quadratic equations or draw cartoons that show the journey of a number through the operations in the order of operations (PEMDAS). Likewise, I've had students work in small groups to compose catchy songs or raps about the properties of triangles or the quadratic formula—a method that turns formulas into memorable musical hooks. This process not only makes content more fun and accessible but also allows students who struggle with traditional assessments to shine creatively while still demonstrating mastery.

Art and music integration isn't limited to math; it can be adapted effectively in any grade or subject. In a second-grade science classroom, for instance, a teacher might have students use watercolors to paint the different stages of a butterfly's life cycle, labeling each phase as they go. Meanwhile, a fourth-grade language arts teacher could ask students to write and perform a short skit or rap based on a chapter from their favorite novel, reinforcing reading comprehension and narrative structure.

In middle school social studies, students might create a mural illustrating major events in state history or work together to compose a folk song about a famous figure. Even in high school chemistry, students could use colored chalk to collaboratively draw complex molecules on the sidewalk outside, allowing them to visualize chemical bonding.

By weaving art and music into academic content, teachers empower students to use their strengths and creativity in the pursuit of learning. This approach not only makes lessons more enjoyable but also sustains enthusiasm for school—helping all students find their voice and solidify connections to what they're learning, no matter the subject or grade level.

Movement-Oriented Activities: Incorporating movement-oriented activities into classroom lessons is a powerful way to boost student energy, engagement, and focus—especially in a subject like math that is often associated with sitting still and working quietly. When students are allowed (and encouraged) to move, they are more alert, their brains are better engaged, and learning often becomes both more effective and enjoyable.

One strategy I regularly use is setting up math relay races where students move around the room to solve problems at different stations. Each team member finishes a problem, then hands off the marker to a classmate, creating a lively and collaborative atmosphere. This not only reinforces concepts we've recently covered but also brings an element of excitement—students are eager to participate, and even those who might be hesitant in a traditional setting are eager to join in.

For geometry, I incorporate physical movement by having students use their arms and bodies to represent different types of angles or geometric transformations. For example, we'll "become" acute, right, or obtuse angles with our arms, or act out rotations and reflections in groups. These kinesthetic methods help students associate concepts with muscle memory, making them easier to recall later.

I also use my classroom's open space for activities like "Math Simon Says," where I call out instructions related to math properties or operations, and students respond with movements. Even simple movement breaks or standing group activities between lessons keep students alert and ready to learn.

These movement-oriented activities not only help solidify understanding but also keep the classroom environment positive and energized. Students walk away not only knowing the material better, but also associating math class with fun, energy, and teamwork—key ingredients for sustained academic motivation and growth.

Think-Pair-Share: Think-Pair-Share is a collaborative strategy that transforms the typical classroom Q&A into a dynamic exercise in collective reasoning and personal engagement. Instead of immediately responding to a question posed by the teacher, students first take a quiet moment to consider their own thoughts and ideas. Next, they pair up with a classmate to discuss their reflections, compare perspectives, and clarify their understanding. Finally, pairs share their combined insights with the whole class, ensuring that every voice has a chance to be heard and that ideas are enriched by multiple viewpoints.

In my classroom, flexible seating adds another layer of effectiveness to Think-Pair-Share. Students aren't confined to traditional desks; they can choose to sit on couches, at high-top tables, or even in gaming chairs. This variety fosters a relaxed and comfortable environment, which encourages students to interact naturally and creatively with their peers during partner discussions. Often, I'll see students seated on the couch leaning in for focused dialogue, or partners at a high-top table jotting ideas on a shared whiteboard, while those in gaming chairs brainstorm with energy and enthusiasm. This physical variety helps students feel empowered and valued, making it easier for even quiet or hesitant learners to participate fully.

Recently, during a lesson on solving word problems in algebra, I posed a challenging scenario for students to solve. First, everyone spent a few minutes jotting down initial strategies in their notebooks. Then, students paired up, using their chosen flexible seating areas to confer and blend their approaches. When we reconvened as a whole group, the quality and depth of solutions shared reflected not just individual thought, but enriched perspectives gained from meaningful peer conversation.

I also use Think-Pair-Share for review sessions, conceptual discussions, and even as a warm-up at the start of class. The combination of collaborative thinking and flexible seating consistently leads to greater student confidence and stronger, more thoughtful responses. By harnessing the benefits of both techniques, I'm able to create an engaging, supportive classroom community where students know their ideas matter—and where every individual is given the space, both physically and intellectually, to succeed.

Flipped-Classroom Approach: The flipped-classroom approach transforms traditional learning by having students engage with new content at home—through videos, readings, or interactive assignments—leaving class time open for deeper exploration and hands-on activities. This model shifts the classroom environment from passive lectures to a vibrant space where students collaborate on problem-solving, participate in small-group discussions, and apply concepts through meaningful projects and debates. It also empowers teachers to deliver more personalized, targeted instruction since class time can be used to address specific questions or misconceptions as they arise.

In my algebra class, implementing the flipped-classroom method has been a game-changer. Before each new unit, I assign short video lessons and guided notes for students to review at their own pace at home. These resources allow students to pause, rewind, and reflect as many times as needed, ensuring they come to class with a foundational understanding. When we meet in person, we dive straight into collaborative activities: working together to solve challenging equations, tackling real-world word problems, or exploring interactive math stations. Instead of listening to lectures, students spend most of their time practicing skills, discussing strategies, and learning from each other.

One reason students genuinely enjoy this method is the sense of ownership and flexibility it provides. They appreciate being able to move through new material at their own speed—skipping what they already know or replaying the parts that are difficult. Class time becomes much more engaging, with a focus on solving interesting problems as a team, getting immediate feedback, and connecting algebraic concepts to practical situations. Many students have told me they feel less anxious asking questions in this collaborative, hands-on setting than in a traditional lecture format. The flipped classroom not only makes learning more active and enjoyable, but it also helps build confidence and a deeper, more lasting understanding of algebra.

Technology-Enhanced Learning: Technology-enhanced learning has become a cornerstone of my teaching practice, bringing energy, personalization, and interactivity to every lesson. The opportunities are virtually limitless—whether students are journeying across countries with Google Earth, collaborating through Nearpod's interactive presentations, or sharing their voices on Flipgrid through creative video responses. These tools make learning feel current and relevant, helping students connect with concepts in ways that a traditional classroom simply can't match.

In my classroom, I use technology every single day to enrich learning experiences. We incorporate virtual field trips to explore mathematical landmarks or real-world applications of algebra, deepening understanding by connecting abstract problems to concrete examples. Students use collaborative online whiteboards to solve equations together in real time, work through interactive simulations to visualize geometric transformations, and participate in live polls to check for understanding or spark engaging debates on problem-solving strategies.

Technology also allows for meaningful differentiation—students can watch tutorial videos at their own pace, access extra practice when needed, or challenge themselves with enrichment activities. I've seen even reluctant learners flourish with these tools, gaining confidence as they find new ways to participate and express their thinking.

By weaving technology seamlessly into daily routines, I not only keep students engaged and motivated, but also prepare them with the digital literacy skills that are vital for future success. The classroom comes alive with curiosity, exploration, and a sense of possibility, as students discover that learning can truly be an interactive and accessible adventure.

By integrating these activities and teaching styles, educators can transform their classrooms into vibrant spaces where students feel excited to learn. Whether through games, movement, storytelling, or technology, the key is to keep learning dynamic, relevant, and engaging. The more students connect with the material, the more they retain—and most importantly, the more they enjoy the journey of education!

Balancing Structure with Creativity and Spontaneity

A great classroom is a place where structure and creativity work hand in hand. Too much structure can stifle imagination, while too much freedom can lead to chaos and confusion. Striking the right balance ensures that students have a solid foundation for learning while also feeling inspired to explore, innovate, and express their ideas. The key is to create an environment where students understand expectations but still have the freedom to think critically and engage in meaningful, creative experiences.

Here's how teachers can successfully blend structure with creativity to maximize student engagement and learning outcomes:

Establishing Clear Objectives and Expectations: Creativity flourishes best when it has a clear direction. Setting learning objectives and classroom expectations gives students a roadmap for success while still allowing them space to explore within defined boundaries. Start each lesson by outlining what students are expected to learn and achieve by the end of the class. Use visual reminders, posted guidelines, and consistent reinforcement to help students stay on track.

However, expectations don't have to be rigid—consider giving students multiple ways to demonstrate their learning. For example, if a history lesson's objective is to explain the causes of the American Revolution, students could write an essay, create a storyboard, or present a dramatic reenactment. Clarity plus flexibility allows students to take ownership of their learning while still working toward a common goal.

Structured Yet Flexible Planning: A well-organized lesson plan provides a framework for learning, but within that structure, there should be room for spontaneity and student-driven exploration. A great way to achieve this is by combining direct instruction with hands-on activities.

For instance, a math teacher might start a lesson with a structured explanation of algebraic equations and then allow students to work on real-world problem-solving projects that require creative thinking. In an English class, students might first analyze a poem's structure and then write their own poetry using different styles and themes. By alternating between structured learning and open-ended activities, teachers keep students engaged while still ensuring academic goals are met.

Guided Inquiry-Based Learning: Inquiry-based learning gives students a sense of autonomy and curiosity, but without structure, it can become aimless. A balanced approach is to provide students with guiding questions, research materials, and a clear timeframe for completion. For example, instead of just telling students to "research an important figure in history," provide specific guiding questions such as:

- *What challenges did this person face?*
- *How did they influence history?*
- *What can we learn from their story today?*

By providing a structured framework, students can pursue topics they're passionate about while still staying focused on the lesson's objectives.

Adaptive Teaching: No matter how well you plan, some of the best teaching moments come spontaneously. Being adaptable allows educators to seize unexpected learning opportunities while still maintaining overall classroom structure.

For instance, if a class discussion about climate change leads to a student asking about renewable energy innovations, take a moment to explore that topic through a brief class debate or quick research activity. This flexibility makes learning feel more relevant and connected to students' interests, fostering deeper engagement.

However, it's important to ensure that these detours still align with overall learning goals. The best adaptive teaching involves recognizing when a spontaneous moment enhances the lesson rather than distracts from it.

Feedback and Reflection: Encouraging students to reflect on their work and providing constructive feedback helps them refine their creativity while staying aligned with academic expectations. Whether it's through class discussions, written reflections, or peer reviews, students need structured opportunities to analyze their own learning experiences. For example, after completing a creative project, ask students:

- *What did you enjoy most about this project?*
- *What challenges did you face, and how did you overcome them?*
- *How does this connect to what we've been learning?*

By making feedback and reflection a regular part of the learning process, students become more intentional about their creativity and develop a deeper understanding of their work.

Routine with Variety: Students thrive on consistency but doing the exact same thing every day can lead to disengagement. A great strategy is to maintain a structured routine while incorporating variety in activities. For example, start every class with a "Question of the Day" to spark curiosity, but change the format—one day it might be a brain teaser, another day a short discussion prompt, and another day a quick interactive game.

Another way to balance routine and variety is through station-based learning, where students rotate through different activities (writing, discussion, hands-on experiment, technology-based research) in one lesson. This keeps things fresh and engaging while maintaining a structured framework.

Creating an Inclusive Environment: A balanced classroom isn't just about structure and creativity—it's also about ensuring all students feel comfortable sharing their ideas. Some students naturally thrive in creative, open-ended activities, while others feel more comfortable with clear structure and step-by-step guidance. To foster inclusivity:

- Offer different ways for students to express their learning (oral presentations, written reflections, creative projects).

- Use collaborative learning so students with different strengths can work together.
- Encourage risk-taking by creating a judgment-free environment where mistakes are seen as part of learning.

When students feel safe, valued, and heard, they're more likely to engage deeply—whether through structured assignments or creative exploration.

Final Thoughts

A classroom that balances structure with creativity is a classroom where students thrive. It ensures that academic rigor is met while still making space for innovation, curiosity, and student expression. When teachers provide clear expectations, flexible planning, guided inquiry, adaptive teaching, regular feedback, varied routines, and an inclusive atmosphere, students are empowered to think critically, take risks, and develop a love for learning.

By embracing both structure and creativity, educators create a classroom culture that is both disciplined and dynamic, where students don't just memorize facts—they actively engage, explore, and grow.

Conclusion: The Journey Toward Everlasting Learning

Creating a fun, energetic learning environment is a blend of structure and spontaneity, where teachers foster curiosity, excitement, and deep engagement while ensuring meaningful learning takes place. Education is more than just delivering content—it's about igniting a passion for discovery, making learning feel like an adventure rather than a task. When students walk into a classroom buzzing with enthusiasm, they don't just absorb information; they actively participate, think critically, and develop a love for learning that extends far beyond the school walls.

An engaging classroom thrives on creativity, where lessons include hands-on experiences, movement-based activities, interactive discussions, and unexpected surprises. Imagine transforming a history lesson into a live reenactment, turning a math class into an escape room challenge, or using music and storytelling to explain scientific concepts. These moments make learning more than just memorization—they make it memorable and meaningful.

But spontaneity doesn't mean chaos—it means being flexible and open to opportunities for deeper learning. Some of the best teaching moments come when teachers allow discussions to take a detour, embrace a student's insightful question, or modify a lesson plan in real-time to better fit the needs and energy of the class. Being adaptable and responsive creates an environment where students feel encouraged to explore, ask questions, and take ownership of their learning.

A lively, energetic classroom has long-term benefits beyond just academic success. When students feel engaged and excited about learning, they develop skills that are critical for real-world success:

- Creativity and Problem-Solving: Engaging, dynamic activities teach students to think outside the box, approach problems from different angles, and embrace new perspectives.
- Collaboration and Communication: Interactive projects, group challenges, and role-playing encourage teamwork, discussion, and confidence in expressing ideas.
- Resilience and Growth Mindset: When learning is fun and interactive, students are more willing to take risks, make mistakes, and persevere, viewing challenges as opportunities for growth.

While spontaneity and creativity add excitement to the classroom, a successful learning environment also requires structure. Establishing clear expectations, routines, and learning goals ensures that creative exploration stays purposeful and productive. Teachers can blend structure with freedom by designing lessons that alternate between focused instruction and hands-on, exploratory learning. For example:

- Start with a structured mini-lesson to introduce key concepts.
- Follow with an interactive, creative activity—such as a debate, hands-on experiment, or group challenge.
- Wrap up with a reflection that helps students connect their learning to broader themes or real-world applications.

By providing a framework that supports creativity, teachers create an atmosphere where students feel safe to explore, experiment, and think independently—all while staying engaged in the learning process.

Despite the challenges that come with balancing structure and creativity, teachers who infuse their classrooms with energy, curiosity, and spontaneity will find the rewards immeasurable. A classroom where students laugh, question, experiment, and explore is one where deep learning happens naturally. When educators approach teaching with enthusiasm and a willingness to adapt and innovate, they transform their classrooms into spaces that spark lifelong curiosity.

The goal isn't just to teach facts—it's to nurture thinkers, creators, and problem-solvers who will carry that love for learning into the future. Through purposeful creativity, dynamic engagement, and a commitment to making learning enjoyable, teachers fulfill one of their most important roles: inspiring students to see knowledge not as an obligation, but as an endless, exciting journey.

Reflection and Action Step

How can I adjust my teaching methods to better meet the diverse learning needs of my students, even if it means stepping outside my own comfort zone?

What is one way I can ensure that students with different learning styles feel supported and included in my classroom?

How do I check that my lesson plans are focused on student growth rather than my own preferred teaching style?

When have I noticed my personal comfort influencing my teaching decisions, and how can I shift my focus back to student needs?

What strategies can I try to better understand the perspectives and challenges faced by students whose learning styles differ from my own?

How will I know if my classroom environment is truly equitable and responsive to all learners, and what steps can I take to improve it if needed??

Action Step

Dedicate time each week to offer students a choice in how they demonstrate their understanding of key concepts.

Chapter 9 - The Role of Accountability for All

Introduction: The Pillar of Educational Success

Accountability is one of the most important factors in creating a classroom culture where both students and teachers take ownership of their roles and responsibilities. It goes beyond simply following rules or completing assignments—it's about fostering a mindset of responsibility, integrity, and growth. When students understand that their actions have consequences, both positive and negative, they become more engaged in their learning. At the same time, when teachers model accountability, they build an atmosphere of trust, fairness, and consistency that encourages students to rise to expectations.

An accountability-driven classroom provides students with clear expectations, guiding them toward taking responsibility for their progress while also ensuring they feel supported. When structured effectively, accountability helps students develop essential life skills, such as time management, self-discipline, and perseverance. It encourages them to reflect on their choices, make adjustments when necessary, and work toward academic and personal goals with a sense of purpose.

For teachers, maintaining accountability means establishing clear guidelines, providing consistent follow-through, and fostering an environment where students understand the importance of personal responsibility. It involves striking the right balance—offering structure and expectations while allowing room for mistakes, learning, and growth. A strong foundation of accountability leads to a positive and constructive classroom experience, where students are motivated to perform at their best and develop habits that extend beyond the classroom.

This chapter will explore the many facets of accountability, examining its impact on student success, teacher effectiveness, and overall classroom dynamics. By understanding how accountability shapes behavior, learning, and personal development, educators can create an environment that promotes responsibility, encourages active participation, and nurtures a lifelong commitment to growth and achievement.

Accountability in the Classroom: A Dual Definition

Accountability in the classroom is a shared commitment between teachers and students, where both play distinct but equally essential roles in maintaining a productive and effective learning environment. For teachers, accountability means more than just delivering lessons— it's about fostering an atmosphere of fairness, consistency, and high expectations. Educators are responsible for designing well-structured lesson plans, providing engaging and relevant instruction, and assessing student progress in a way that is transparent and constructive. They must also ensure that classroom policies are enforced consistently and equitably, setting the tone for a space where students feel supported yet challenged.

Beyond instructional duties, teachers have an obligation to adapt to students' needs, create inclusive spaces, and offer meaningful feedback that encourages growth. Whether through personalized instruction, timely grading, or clear communication, an accountable teacher models professionalism and integrity—demonstrating to students what responsibility looks like in action. By holding themselves to a high standard, educators inspire students to take their own role in learning seriously.

For students, accountability is about taking ownership of their education. This means showing up prepared, completing assignments on time, engaging actively in discussions, and embracing both successes and challenges as part of the learning process. A responsible student recognizes that their effort, discipline, and participation directly influence their academic outcomes. They understand that accountability is not just about following rules but about developing the skills and mindset necessary for long-term success—both in school and in life.

One feature that adds a practical and motivating layer to accountability in my classroom is our classroom economic system, centered on "Carpenter Cash." As students demonstrate responsibility—whether it's participating in discussions, helping a classmate, completing assignments on time, or showing leadership— they have the chance to earn Carpenter Cash. This currency can be exchanged for a variety of incentives, such as snacks, extra computer time, homework passes, or other privileges. However, accountability works in both directions: students can also be fined for actions like missing assignments, off-task behavior, or not following classroom guidelines.

This system makes the abstract concept of accountability tangible and meaningful for students. They quickly learn that their choices have real, immediate consequences, both positive and negative. The economic aspect motivates students not just to meet expectations, but to strive for consistency in their actions and decisions. It teaches them real-life skills about responsibility, consequences, budgeting, and delayed gratification—skills that extend far beyond the classroom.

When teachers and students work together in an atmosphere of mutual accountability, especially with tools like the classroom economic system in place, the classroom becomes a dynamic space of trust, motivation, and collaboration. Teachers provide the framework and guidance, ensuring a structured environment, while students take charge of their learning journey. This partnership isn't just about rules—it's about building character, fostering engagement and achievement, and equipping students for personal and academic growth.

Clarity of Expectations: Setting clear expectations eliminates confusion and ensures that students fully understand their academic and behavioral responsibilities. Teachers should outline classroom rules, performance standards, and participation expectations at the beginning of the year and revisit them frequently. These expectations should be written down, displayed, and reinforced through discussion and practice.

For example, instead of simply saying, "Homework must be completed on time," specify, "Homework is due at the beginning of class. Late submissions will receive a 10% deduction per day unless prior arrangements have been made." The more specific the expectations, the easier it is for students to adhere to them and take ownership of their responsibilities.

Additionally, discussing the "why" behind classroom expectations helps students understand their purpose. When students recognize that deadlines prepare them for real-world responsibilities or that active participation enhances their learning experience, they are more likely to comply with expectations not just out of obligation but out of understanding.

Designated Rules and Responsibilities: Designated Rules and Responsibilities: Rules should be clearly defined, fair, and relevant to both academic success and classroom conduct. Establishing these guidelines collaboratively by involving students in the rule-setting process fosters greater investment and accountability. When students have a say in creating the classroom norms, they are more likely to respect and follow them. For example, rather than dictating all the rules, teachers might ask students:

- *What behaviors help create a positive learning environment?*
- *What should happen if someone disrupts the learning process?*

This collaborative approach helps students internalize the rules as a shared commitment rather than an imposed structure. Additionally, regularly revisiting and discussing these norms ensures that they remain fresh and meaningful throughout the school year.

Responsibilities should also be clearly assigned within the classroom. Whether it's rotating roles for classroom tasks, setting peer mentoring systems, or assigning group leaders for projects, giving students specific duties helps build a culture of accountability. When students know their role in maintaining the classroom environment, they become more engaged and responsible for its success.

In my classroom, the foundation of our expectations is built upon five guiding "Be" statements: Be prepared, be respectful, be responsible, be positive, and be electronic-device-free. These straightforward yet comprehensive guidelines provide clear direction and set a tone of mutual respect and readiness to learn. At the beginning of the year, I engage students in discussions about what each "Be" statement means and how their actions can support these principles in practice. We brainstorm examples and non-examples and collectively discuss potential consequences for not adhering to our shared standards.

To reinforce and motivate adherence to these "Be" statements, I employ our classroom economic system—Carpenter Cash. By consistently meeting these expectations, students earn Carpenter Cash which can be redeemed for privileges and rewards. Conversely, lapses such as tardiness or inappropriate device use may result in fines. This system offers immediate feedback, celebrates positive choices, and encourages a sense of personal responsibility. The combination of collaboratively established rules, clearly defined roles, and a motivating reward system creates a supportive and accountable classroom culture where every student is empowered to contribute to our collective success.

Regular Monitoring and Feedback: Accountability is reinforced through consistent monitoring and feedback. Teachers should have systems in place to track student progress, participation, and behavior—whether through grades, check-ins, observation, or student reflections. Regular feedback helps students recognize their strengths and identify areas for improvement, keeping them accountable for their learning journey.

However, feedback should be timely, constructive, and growth-oriented. Instead of simply pointing out mistakes, teachers should provide actionable steps for improvement. For example:

- Instead of: "Your essay lacked organization."
- Try: "Your essay presents strong ideas, but restructuring your paragraphs to follow a clearer sequence will improve readability. Let's discuss how to outline your points effectively."

Teachers should also encourage self-assessment and peer feedback, which allows students to actively reflect on their work and develop a sense of responsibility for their learning progress. Simple strategies such as self-evaluation checklists or peer review sessions can help students recognize their accountability in meeting learning standards.

Consistent Enforcement of Rules: Fairness and consistency are essential when it comes to enforcing classroom rules. If expectations are not applied consistently, students may become confused or feel that consequences are arbitrary. For instance, if one student is penalized for talking out of turn but another is ignored for the same behavior, it creates a sense of injustice that can undermine classroom morale. To maintain fairness, teachers should:

- Apply rules equally to all students without favoritism.
- Address infractions immediately and consistently rather than selectively enforcing rules.
- Be transparent about expectations and the reasons behind consequences.

However, consistency does not mean rigidity. Teachers should use context and discretion when applying rules. A student who occasionally forgets an assignment due to unforeseen circumstances should not be treated the same as a student who repeatedly neglects responsibilities. By balancing compassion with accountability, educators maintain a fair and structured environment that students respect.

Role of Consequences: Role of Consequences: Consequences should be seen as learning opportunities rather than punishments. The goal is not to instill fear but to help students understand the importance of their actions and encourage better decision-making in the future. Effective consequences are clear, proportionate, and connected to the behavior in question.

Instead of relying solely on punitive measures, I embrace restorative approaches that help students reflect, grow, and improve. For example:

- If a student misses a deadline, I don't just deduct points; I ask them to reflect on their time management, set a new goal, and provide an opportunity to submit improved work.
- If a student disrupts class, rather than assigning detention, I initiate a conversation about the impact of their behavior on the learning environment. Through this dialogue, students begin to see how their actions affect others and the community as a whole.

Clear and fair consequences help students internalize accountability, teaching them that their choices have real outcomes while also offering a path toward growth and improvement. Restorative discipline emphasizes reflection and responsibility, nurturing skills students carry into all aspects of their lives. This positive, forward-looking approach helps build a culture of trust, respect, and empathy—qualities essential for long-term success.

A pivotal component in my classroom is the Carpenter Cash economic system, which further reinforces the connection between actions and outcomes. Students are rewarded for meeting expectations, completing assignments, demonstrating kindness, or taking on leadership roles. Conversely, inappropriate behaviors or missed responsibilities may result in a fine. However, rather than simply punishing, I use these moments as teachable opportunities—students might "pay" a fine but are also encouraged to reflect, discuss alternative choices, and earn their way back through positive actions.

This system brings real-life relevance to the concept of consequences—students quickly learn that every decision, big or small, has tangible effects. But most importantly, the emphasis remains on learning, improvement, and reclaiming responsibility, rather than shame or punishment.

Altogether, accountability thrives in a classroom where expectations are clear, consequences are constructive, and every moment is a chance to grow. By combining restorative discipline with practical systems like Carpenter Cash, I foster a structured, supportive environment where students are empowered to develop self-discipline, responsibility, and integrity—building the foundation they need for lifelong learning and achievement.

Self-assessment: Implement self-assessment practices where students reflect on their learning journey and identify areas needing improvement on their own. By engaging in self-evaluation, students develop critical thinking and self-awareness, becoming more attuned to their educational responsibilities. Teachers can facilitate this process through reflective journals, student-led conferences, or learning portfolios.

Even without using journals, there are many practical ways I guide my students in self-assessing their progress in algebra. Throughout lessons, I often incorporate rubrics or checklists that align directly with our learning targets. After completing a task, students reflect on their performance by rating themselves for each criterion—such as how accurately they solved an equation or whether they clearly showed all their steps. This process helps them recognize their strengths and areas needing improvement, all without the need for lengthy written explanations.

Hand signals offer another immediate form of self-assessment. At various points during class, I'll ask students to indicate their confidence in a concept with their hands—five fingers for complete understanding down to a fist for total confusion. This allows for honest, low-pressure reflection, and gives me and the students instant feedback about the general comfort level in the room.

Exit tickets are also a staple in my classroom. At the end of a lesson or activity, students respond to a targeted question such as, "What's one thing you understand well about graphing linear equations?" or "What was the hardest step in today's problem-solving process?" These tickets can be verbal, on paper, or digital, and provide students with quick and meaningful opportunities to assess their own understanding.

On assignments, I always include the day's learning target and have students indicate, often by circling or coloring, how well they feel they've grasped the skill—from "I do not understand at all" to "I could teach someone else." This visual approach to self-reflection makes it easy for students to monitor and communicate their progress.

Peer discussions and turn-and-talks are another powerful tool; students share with a partner what they found most challenging or easy about the lesson or explain their thinking when solving a problem. These conversations foster metacognition and let students learn from one another, making self-assessment less intimidating.

Occasionally, I use quick classroom polling—with technology or simply a show of hands—to gauge how confident everyone feels, or which topics need more attention. This informal check empowers students to reflect on their understanding in real time.

Peer Support Systems: Peer support and tutoring are cornerstones of my classroom environment, not only because they promote collaboration, but also because they foster deeper learning and mutual accountability. As research and experience show, students develop stronger understanding and greater confidence when they are required to explain concepts to others. (Mazur, 1997) In my classroom, I actively nurture these dynamics by incorporating a peer tutoring system where students support each other's learning and growth.

To motivate and recognize this valuable work, I use our classroom currency, Carpenter Cash, as an incentive. When a student volunteers to tutor a classmate or lead a study group, they earn Carpenter Cash for their time and effort. This not only formalizes the value of their contribution but also adds a fun, real-world dimension to the tutoring process. Students who need extra help know their peers are available and eager to connect, creating a culture of support rather than competition.

The impact of this is profound. I've seen students who may not have excelled in traditional tests truly shine when they take on the role of tutor. Explaining how to solve a challenging algebraic equation, for example, reinforces their own understanding and builds their communication skills. Often, students report that teaching a new topic to a peer helped them see the concept from a new angle—clarifying gaps in their knowledge and solidifying their grasp on the material.

Receiving peer support is just as transformative. A student struggling with factoring polynomials may feel more comfortable asking questions and practicing with a classmate than in a whole group setting. This personalized attention supports differentiated instruction and gives every learner a pathway to success.

Carpenter Cash, as a reward for tutoring, adds another level of engagement. Earning this currency not only provides tangible recognition but also allows students to access other class rewards, making participation in peer tutoring both intrinsically and extrinsically motivating.

Through this system, peer support becomes woven into the fabric of our classroom—strengthening individual confidence, deepening content understanding, and nurturing a collaborative learning community where everyone has something valuable to offer.

Celebrating Achievements: Celebrating achievements is an essential part of building a positive and motivating classroom culture. When students meet goals or go above and beyond expectations, I make it a priority to recognize their hard work and growth. Positive reinforcement not only boosts individual morale but also encourages others to strive for excellence and maintain accountability. It turns each success—big or small—into a meaningful moment that instills pride and confidence.

In my classroom, celebrations are woven into our daily and weekly routines. We use Carpenter Cash as a reward system, and students earn it not just for academic success but also for acts of kindness, improvement, or teamwork. For example, after a challenging algebra unit, I recently recognized a student who had set a goal to raise his quiz scores by consistently practicing at home and asking questions during class. When he finally achieved his goal, the class celebrated with a spontaneous round of applause, and he received Carpenter Cash that he could redeem for a favorite snack or extra computer free time.

I also make a point to honor achievements publicly—such as highlighting "Math Stars of the Week" on our bulletin board or holding small celebrations for classes that reach collective goals, like 100% homework completion. These moments not only motivate individual students but also build a sense of community. Students begin to see that their efforts matter, and that both their personal growth and their contributions to the class are valued. Ultimately, celebrating achievements keeps students driven and eager to reach new heights in their learning journey.

Cultivating a Growth Mindset: Cultivating a growth mindset is at the core of helping students not only achieve academically but also develop resilience and accountability in all aspects of their lives. In my classroom, I explicitly teach that intelligence and abilities are not fixed but can be expanded with consistent effort and perseverance. This shift in mindset transforms challenges from intimidating barriers into valuable opportunities for discovery and development.

Whenever students encounter difficult material or make mistakes, I encourage them to see these experiences as essential steps in the learning process. We regularly discuss how even the most successful mathematicians and scientists faced failures but used them as launching pads for growth. I model this attitude by sharing my own experiences of overcoming obstacles and the effort it took to master new skills.

For example, during a particularly tough algebra topic, I remind students that struggling with a concept doesn't mean they "aren't good at math" but that their brains are simply doing the hard work of learning something new. I praise persistence and celebrate small improvements, emphasizing the value of steady progress over immediate perfection.

By fostering a growth mindset, I see students become more willing to take risks, ask questions, and be proactive about their learning. They start holding themselves accountable, persevering through setbacks, and developing a lifelong belief that dedication and effort can lead to meaningful success. This mindset not only empowers them in math but also gives them tools to face future challenges with confidence.

Conclusion: Accountability as the Cornerstone of Classroom Success

Accountability is indispensable in fostering an environment of trust, respect, and high expectations within the classroom. By clearly defining accountability for teachers and students, setting transparent rules and responsibilities, and promoting self-directed learning through goal setting, self-assessment, and peer support, educators pave the path for academic and personal success.

Accountability is more than an administrative necessity; it is a vital ethos that enriches the educational experience. As students grow and understand their roles within this shared responsibility framework, they develop skills and attributes that not only serve their academic endeavors but extend to their future personal and professional lives. Thus, instilling accountability ensures that students become conscientious, responsible citizens equipped with the values needed to navigate and contribute to an unpredictable and complex world. As such, accountability remains a central and unifying force in the pursuit of educational excellence for all.

Reflection and Action Step

How do you demonstrate responsibility and integrity in your daily interactions with students, and what impact do you notice this has on classroom culture?

What specific strategies do you use to communicate expectations to students, and how do you ensure that all students understand them?

Describe a time when you followed through with a consequence or reward in your classroom. What did you learn from this experience about maintaining consistency?

In what ways do you create opportunities for students to reflect on their choices and adjust their learning behaviors? How do you support them through this process?

How do you balance giving students structure and autonomy, and what adjustments have you made when this balance wasn't working?

What feedback have you received from students about accountability in your classroom, and how have you used this feedback to improve your approach??

Action Step

Designate time each week for students and yourself to share one example of accountability—the challenges faced and strategies used to overcome them. Invite students to describe how they took responsibility and what they learned, while you model this reflection yourself. This practice encourages open dialogue, strengthens responsibility, and builds a classroom culture centered on growth.

Chapter 10 - The Principle of Success Encourages More Success

Introduction: The Virtuous Cycle of Success

Success is not just an endpoint; it is a dynamic process that, once initiated, tends to perpetuate itself. The principle of "success encourages more success" operates on a simple yet powerful theorem: achievement breeds further motivation and leads to successive accomplishments. This concept is deeply rooted in psychological theories that elucidate how the reinforcement of success acts as a catalyst for continued efforts. This chapter explores the psychological foundations of the success cycle, demonstrates its impact through case studies, and discusses strategies to create opportunities for success that accommodate individual student strengths and challenges.

Psychological Foundations of the Success Cycle

The psychological underpinnings of the success cycle are largely based on reinforcement theories and intrinsic motivation. Broadly speaking, achieving a particular goal or milestone generates a positive emotional and cognitive response that reinforces the desire to pursue further goals. This invigorates a cycle where perceived success boosts confidence, prompting individuals to set and achieve even greater goals.

Self-Efficacy: The theory of self-efficacy, developed by renowned psychologist Albert Bandura, centers on the fundamental belief individuals hold about their own capabilities to effectively carry out behaviors required to achieve specific goals or performance outcomes. (Bandura, 1997) This belief is not simply about possessing particular skills; rather, it focuses on an individual's confidence in their ability to utilize those skills successfully in varying contexts and situations.

Self-efficacy significantly influences multiple dimensions of human functioning, including emotional responses, cognitive processes, motivational patterns, and behavioral choices. People with high self-efficacy tend to approach challenging tasks proactively, view difficulties as opportunities to grow, and persist longer in the face of obstacles. This persistence often leads to enhanced performance and accomplishment, creating a positive cycle of achievement and increased self-belief.

Conversely, individuals who doubt their capabilities frequently perceive challenges as insurmountable obstacles, causing them to avoid tasks, quickly lose motivation, or abandon efforts when faced with adversity. Such experiences reinforce negative perceptions of their abilities, perpetuating a cycle of decreased performance and further diminishing self-confidence.

Central to Bandura's concept is the idea that successful experiences are essential in fostering stronger self-efficacy. When people experience accomplishments, even minor ones, their confidence in their abilities is reinforced, leading to higher motivation and improved future performance. Thus, self-efficacy acts as a powerful determinant of personal growth and achievement, shaping how individuals set goals, approach challenges, and ultimately realize their potential across diverse areas of their lives.

Intrinsic Motivation: Intrinsic motivation, as conceptualized within Edward Deci and Richard Ryan's self-determination theory, represents the internal drive to engage in activities for their inherent satisfaction and enjoyment, rather than for external rewards or pressures. (Ryan & Deci, 2017) This theory emphasizes that intrinsic motivation is a critical component in fostering self-regulated and autonomous behavior. Individuals driven by intrinsic motivation actively seek out and engage in activities purely for the pleasure and personal fulfillment they derive from them, rather than due to external incentives or requirements.

Deci and Ryan identify three core psychological needs essential for cultivating intrinsic motivation: competence, autonomy, and relatedness. Competence refers to a person's belief in their capability to effectively accomplish tasks and meet challenges. Autonomy involves having a sense of personal control and choice in one's actions, where individuals feel they are the originators of their own behavior rather than feeling controlled by external factors. Relatedness encompasses the desire to connect meaningfully with others, fostering a sense of belonging and interpersonal engagement.

When these psychological needs are met, individuals experience enhanced intrinsic motivation, increasing their engagement, persistence, and overall satisfaction in their endeavors. Experiences of success particularly bolster feelings of competence and autonomy, reinforcing an individual's internal motivation and prompting further pursuit of similar rewarding activities. This self-sustaining cycle of fulfillment and achievement contributes significantly to personal growth and continuous learning.

Conversely, when individuals lack opportunities to experience competence, autonomy, or relatedness, their intrinsic motivation diminishes. They may begin to rely more heavily on external rewards or coercion, resulting in reduced persistence, decreased satisfaction, and poorer long-term performance.

Thus, Deci and Ryan's self-determination theory highlights the profound importance of intrinsic motivation in personal development and performance, advocating environments that foster autonomy, competence, and relatedness to maximize individual fulfillment and effectiveness.

The dopamine feedback loop: The dopamine feedback loop, a concept rooted deeply in neuroscience, provides insight into how human motivation and behavior are biologically reinforced through neurological processes. (Glimcher, 2011) At its core, this mechanism involves dopamine—a neurotransmitter widely recognized for its role in generating feelings of pleasure, reward, and satisfaction. When individuals achieve a goal or experience success, their brains release dopamine, which subsequently generates a strong sense of gratification and enjoyment. This biochemical reward not only produces immediate pleasure but also establishes a neurological pattern that influences future behavior.

The release of dopamine reinforces the specific actions that led to the success, thereby motivating individuals to repeat similar behaviors. This cyclical process creates what is known as the dopamine feedback loop, essentially wiring the brain to seek out and engage in activities that produce these rewarding experiences. Over time, repeated exposure to success and the corresponding dopamine release strengthens the neural pathways associated with achievement-oriented behaviors, making them more likely to recur and become habitual.

This neurochemical mechanism can profoundly impact personal motivation, learning, and goal-setting strategies. As dopamine reinforces certain behaviors, individuals naturally become more inclined to pursue tasks or challenges that have previously resulted in positive outcomes. Consequently, the dopamine feedback loop significantly shapes how people approach their ambitions, influencing their resilience, perseverance, and overall drive toward success. Understanding the dopamine feedback loop is crucial not only in neuroscience but also in practical applications, including education, personal development, and organizational management. By intentionally designing tasks and environments that facilitate experiences of achievement, it is possible to leverage this powerful neurological process to enhance motivation, productivity, and sustained engagement.

Case Studies and Anecdotes: From Small Successes to Big Achievements

Success, whether small or large, acts as the steppingstone toward greater accomplishments. Real-life experiences highlighting how incremental wins lead to larger victories provide compelling testimony to this principle.

Academic Journeys: Consider the academic journey of a student who initially struggles with mathematics, viewing the subject as intimidating and beyond their grasp. With patient guidance and consistent encouragement from a dedicated teacher, the student gradually masters foundational mathematical concepts, leading to noticeable improvements on standardized assessments. Each small triumph reinforces their self-belief, gradually transforming their mindset and approach to learning.

Buoyed by newfound confidence from these initial successes, the student willingly embraces more complex and challenging mathematical concepts. Their increased proficiency opens doors to advanced coursework, and soon mathematics becomes not merely manageable but genuinely enjoyable. With each incremental achievement, the student's motivation and self-efficacy deepen, creating a powerful feedback loop of success and confidence. Eventually, what began as a series of modest academic victories evolves into substantial educational accomplishments, laying a strong foundation for further scholarly pursuits.

This progression underscores the importance of recognizing and celebrating small achievements within educational contexts. Incremental successes build resilience, enhance self-esteem, and foster sustained engagement, ultimately propelling students toward significant accomplishments they once deemed impossible.

Athletic Accomplishments: An aspiring athlete determines to reduce their race time. At the beginning of their training journey, the athlete sets modest yet achievable goals. Each time they achieve a new personal record, however minor, they experience an undeniable boost in confidence and motivation. This heightened motivation encourages the athlete to persistently refine their training routines, enhance their techniques, and intensify their commitment.

As weeks and months pass, these incremental improvements accumulate. Techniques become sharper, stamina increases, and overall performance steadily improves. Each small success serves as powerful psychological reinforcement, solidifying the athlete's belief in their capacity for excellence. The athlete begins to recognize that what initially seemed like small advancements have compounded into substantial gains.

Eventually, the athlete's improved performance opens doors to more competitive opportunities. They find themselves qualifying for higher-level competitions and challenging opponents who once seemed unbeatable. This elevated exposure inspires even greater determination, perpetuating a cycle of continuous improvement and achievement.

This narrative highlights how each incremental success—each minor personal best—plays a crucial role in building toward significant athletic accomplishments. Through consistent effort, persistent training, and strategic refinements motivated by successive small victories, the athlete transforms modest beginnings into remarkable achievements. Thus, athletic endeavors exemplify how sustained commitment to incremental progress can ultimately lead to extraordinary success.

Career Development: Success, whether small or large, acts as the steppingstone toward greater accomplishments. Real-life experiences highlighting how incremental wins lead to larger victories provide compelling testimony to this principle. In the realm of career development, this concept is particularly evident. Imagine an individual who begins their professional journey by successfully completing modest, clearly defined workplace projects. With each small project accomplished effectively and efficiently, the employee garners positive attention and appreciation from supervisors and team leaders. Recognition of these achievements gradually translates into enhanced trust and respect within the organization.

As this individual's reliability and competence become more apparent, management increasingly entrusts them with responsibilities of greater complexity and significance. Over time, their role expands from routine tasks to pivotal assignments, enabling the development of new skills and competencies. Each successful project not only enhances the individual's reputation but also significantly boosts their confidence, driving them to seek even greater challenges.

Eventually, this series of incremental successes culminates in substantial career progression opportunities, such as promotions, leadership roles, or critical inclusion in influential projects. This professional trajectory clearly demonstrates the reinforcing effect initial accomplishments have on subsequent opportunities. Success breeds confidence, competence, and recognition, which, in turn, facilitate more profound professional growth.

Thus, small achievements act as leverage points, progressively building a strong foundation for career advancement. By consistently delivering quality outcomes in smaller responsibilities, professionals position themselves favorably for future success. This real-world illustration reinforces the understanding that sustained career advancement emerges from a pattern of incremental accomplishments, demonstrating the transformative power of modest, consistent success.

Strategies for Creating Opportunities for Success

Educators and mentors play a pivotal role in constructing pathways to success by aligning tasks with student strengths and gauging development opportunities. Tailoring experiences for individual success fosters long-term growth.

Individualized Goal Setting: Educators have a profound opportunity—and responsibility—to create environments where all students can experience genuine success. One of the most effective ways to do this is through individualized goal setting. By customizing goals for each student based on their unique strengths, interests, and areas for growth, educators help ensure that each learner faces not only achievable challenges but also meaningful ones. When students see their progress and accomplishments reflected in goals that resonate personally, success becomes more tangible, motivating, and self-reinforcing.

Tailoring learning experiences is more than just recognizing students' differences; it's an active process of observation, communication, and adaptation. For long-term growth, it's important that goals aren't just attainable in the short term—they should also equip students with the skills, confidence, and resilience to tackle future challenges. This could involve differentiating assessments, offering choice in how students demonstrate their learning, or providing varied supports based on individual needs. When students understand that their goals are not arbitrary but are designed specifically for their development, it fosters a stronger sense of ownership and agency over their educational journey.

Consider an example from my own classroom. At the beginning of each term, I sit down with each student to discuss their previous progress, interests, and areas they wish to improve. Together, we set personalized academic and behavioral goals. For instance, one student who excelled in creative writing but struggled with organization set a goal to complete graphic organizers for each writing assignment. With regular check-ins, guided feedback, and incremental supports, the student gradually became more independent in planning their work—eventually expressing pride in their own organizational growth.

Another example involves a student who was highly capable in math but lacked confidence presenting solutions to the class. We set a goal for them to share their reasoning in small groups before progressing to whole-class presentations. These small, personalized steps transformed what was initially a source of anxiety into a genuine area of achievement.

By continually customizing goals and supports, I help each student discover that success is not a one-size-fits-all destination. Instead, it's a journey marked by personal effort, growth, and the realization that their unique path matters. This approach doesn't just help students achieve academically—it also builds lifelong skills in self-advocacy, perseverance, and self-reflection, setting the foundation for continued growth long after they leave my classroom.

Scaffolded Learning: Scaffolded learning is especially impactful in subjects like math and algebra, where complex concepts can often seem overwhelming without structured support. By breaking difficult topics and problems into smaller, more manageable steps, educators create a pathway of immediate milestones that not only build foundational skills but also nurture a student's confidence as they work through increasingly difficult challenges. Each small success becomes a building block, empowering students to tackle more advanced material with less anxiety and increased self-assurance.

Effective scaffolding in math goes beyond simply offering hints or checking for the right answer—it involves anticipating common struggles and structuring lessons so that each new idea or skill is introduced incrementally. For example, the process might start with visual aids, guided practice, or hands-on activities before transitioning to independent work. Teachers also differentiate support based on individual needs, gradually removing these supports as students gain proficiency. This responsive approach helps students feel supported but not dependent, allowing them to experience authentic accomplishment at every stage.

In my own algebra class, I see the power of scaffolding regularly. Take, for instance, teaching students to solve systems of equations—a notoriously challenging topic for many. Instead of launching directly into word problems or multiple-step equations, I start by ensuring students are comfortable with the basics: understanding what a system is and solving simple problems by graphing. Once this is mastered, we move on to substitution and elimination methods, with each technique broken down into its own clear, sequential steps, supported by worked examples and collaborative practice.

For a recent unit, I had students first identify the solution to a system by seeing where two lines cross on a graph—reinforcing the visual concept before adding in the algebraic process. As confidence grew, we integrated real-world problems, walking through scenarios together and highlighting familiar patterns. One student, who initially found systems of equations daunting, remarked how each small win—like correctly setting up the equations or recognizing parallel lines—helped her feel "ready for the next level." By the end of the unit, she was confidently solving mixed-method problems independently.

Scaffolded learning in my math class is about making sure no one is left behind at any step. Through carefully structured tasks and ongoing encouragement, I help my students transform challenges into opportunities for steady progress, achievement, and, ultimately, a lifelong confidence in their mathematical abilities.

Positive Feedback and Recognition: Providing timely and specific positive feedback is a cornerstone of building success in any classroom, and it holds particular significance in an 8th-grade math or algebra setting. When educators offer genuine recognition for students' accomplishments—no matter how small—it reinforces a growth mindset and makes the path to success feel accessible for every learner. Celebrating both big and incremental achievements creates an uplifting atmosphere where effort and improvement are valued, not just perfection or speed. This approach supports students' morale and links hard work with positive outcomes, increasing their intrinsic motivation to push through challenges.

Effective positive feedback is about much more than saying "good job." It involves noticing the details of a student's work, acknowledging specific progress, and reflecting back the strategies or thinking that led to their success. For example, rather than generically praising a correct answer, an educator might highlight the logical steps a student took or the creative approach they used to solve a problem. This helps students internalize what strategies work well, encouraging them to replicate successful behaviors in future tasks. Consistent recognition builds a sense of belonging and investment, and even modest accomplishments can be meaningful markers of growth, especially for students who may be struggling.

In my 8th-grade algebra class, I strive to make positive feedback an everyday practice. When a student who traditionally struggles with factoring finally succeeds in breaking down a quadratic expression, I make a point to offer specific praise: "I noticed how you carefully checked the signs in each step and didn't rush—your attention to detail paid off!" At the end of each week, I also spotlight individual "math moments"—such as a student making a breakthrough during a group activity or showing persistence on a tough homework set—by sharing their story with the class. Sometimes we even write quick notes of encouragement for classmates, posting them on our "Wall of Wins."

Recently, a student who was apprehensive about graphing linear equations received a round of applause after successfully plotting a line for the first time. His confidence soared, and he later told me, "I felt like I actually belonged in algebra." Experiences like these show that, when positive feedback is specific and celebratory, it not only reinforces learning but also transforms students' attitudes toward math. By recognizing and celebrating progress at every turn, I help foster an environment where students believe in their ongoing potential and are eager to pursue new mathematical challenges.

Encouraging a Growth Mindset: Teaching and fostering a growth mindset is fundamental to student success, especially in challenging subjects like 8th-grade math. Drawing on Carol Dweck's research, I continually promote the belief that intelligence and abilities are not static; rather, they can be developed and strengthened through sustained effort, deliberate practice, and perseverance (Dweck 2007). Rather than viewing mistakes or difficulties as evidence of inadequacy,

I help students understand that these experiences are crucial steppingstones on the path to mastery. By consistently encouraging effort, resilience, and adaptability, I lay the groundwork for students to persist in the face of setbacks and to realize that true success is a continuous journey of learning and growth.

In my classroom, I often reframe challenges as opportunities for development. I celebrate "productive struggle"—when students wrestle with difficult problems and refuse to give up—by highlighting the value of persistence. We discuss famous mathematicians and scientists who encountered failure and learned from it. When a student gets stuck, I encourage them to ask themselves, "What am I learning from this mistake?" or "Which strategy can I try next?" This practice shifts their focus from immediate correctness to long-term improvement, reducing anxiety and self-doubt.

For instance, during our unit on solving equations, I noticed many students grew frustrated after making calculation errors. Instead of letting them feel defeated, I invited the class to share common mistakes and brainstorm together how to check their work and use errors as clues for understanding concepts more deeply. One student, who struggled with negative numbers, began to approach each problem with curiosity—wondering not "Did I get it right?" but "What does this teach me about the process?" Over time, I observed her confidence and willingness to tackle new problems grow significantly.

At the start of each unit, I invite students to set "learning goals" that prioritize effort-based objectives, like "I will try two new problem-solving strategies this week," or "I'll ask a question whenever I'm stuck." We track progress alongside achievement, so students see growth as multifaceted and not just tied to grades. Feedback in my class is centered around their strategies and persistence, not just the final answers.

By teaching and modeling a growth mindset, I help my students see that every step—success or setback—is part of their development as mathematicians. This approach not only supports better academic outcomes, but it also prepares students for lifelong success by nurturing confidence, adaptability, and a love of learning they can carry far beyond my classroom (Dweck 2007).

Creating Supportive Communities: Creating supportive communities within the classroom is vital for student success, particularly in a subject like math where collaboration can make challenging concepts more approachable. By nurturing an environment where peer support and teamwork are valued, I help ensure that students not only work toward individual goals but also learn to celebrate and contribute to the success of others. This dynamic disperses the traditional, isolated path to achievement and instead builds a culture in which shared encouragement strengthens everyone's growth.

Fostering such a community involves intentionally designing activities that require collaboration and communication. I routinely arrange students into pairs or small groups for problem-solving tasks, encouraging them to share their thinking processes, identify alternative strategies, and help each other when stuck. Students quickly come to see that asking for assistance is a strength, not a weakness, and that explaining their reasoning helps deepen their understanding as well. The collective sense of responsibility leads students to cheer for one another's successes and offer support when someone is struggling.

In my math classroom, I see the benefits of a supportive community every day. For example, during our algebra units, I implement "math partner days," where students tackle multi-step problems together. One recent session involved students working in groups to solve equations and then teach the method to another group. I observed how quieter students found the confidence to share ideas in a smaller setting, while higher-achieving students refined their understanding by explaining concepts to peers. Celebrating group achievements—such as solving a particularly challenging problem or reaching a class-wide goal—further strengthens our sense of unity.

When students feel a part of a supportive learning community, they're more willing to persevere through difficult tasks and genuinely celebrate each other's progress. This collaborative spirit transforms math challenges into shared victories, building not just academic skills but also relationships and resilience that last beyond the classroom.

Adaptation and Reflection: Adaptation and reflection are integral components of a dynamic learning environment, especially in my math classroom where student growth is both celebrated and continuously sought after. By fostering opportunities for regular self-assessment and reflection, I empower students to become active participants in their learning process. When students track their efforts, analyze their outcomes, and thoughtfully consider both successes and setbacks, they become more aware of their own progress. This self-awareness encourages them to adopt adaptive strategies, leading to incremental successes that gradually build toward major achievements.

To make reflection meaningful, I integrate it into our daily and weekly routines. After completing a quiz or tackling a challenging problem set, I ask students to review their work and answer guided reflection questions, such as "What strategy did I use?", "What worked well for me?", and "Where did I get stuck?" This practice isn't about assigning blame or focusing solely on errors—it's about encouraging honest evaluation and helping students recognize patterns in their thinking and work habits.

In my classroom, I've seen the positive impact of this approach. During our algebra unit on linear equations, I introduced math journals where students recorded not only their answers but also their methods and reflections on the process. One student initially struggled with distributing negatives but, through regular self-assessment, began to identify this as a recurring issue. After becoming conscious of this pattern, she made a habit of double-checking these steps and, over time, saw her accuracy and confidence increase significantly. Watching her incremental improvements add up to a breakthrough on the unit test was a powerful reminder of how small reflections can lead to major victories.

By making adaptation and reflection a core part of learning, I help students take ownership of their educational journey, equipping them with the tools to adjust their strategies, celebrate their progress, and continually aim higher.

Conclusion: Sustaining the Momentum of Success

Undoubtedly, once fostered, the momentum of success is profound and virtuous, illuminating a path toward further achievement. By understanding and exploiting the psychological tenets that drive this cycle, and by thoughtfully engineering learning experiences, educators and mentors can critically enhance aspirational pathways for students.

Success is not merely a destination; it is a continuous process that establishes a robust foundation for lifelong learning and achievement. With every small accomplishment propelling the pursuit of larger goals, students not only outperform former benchmarks but also acquire the resilience and empowerment needed to navigate life's broader challenges. Through strategic cultivation of this principle, an encompassing framework for personal achievement can be established, ultimately nurturing a generation of individuals who are both enterprising and self-motivated.

Reflection and Action Step

How do I intentionally design lessons and interactions to ensure that real learning—not just content coverage—occurs for every student?

In what ways am I adapting my teaching strategies to meet the unique needs and learning styles of each student in my classroom?

How do I create a classroom environment where every student feels valued, supported, and empowered to take intellectual risks?

What steps do I take to cultivate curiosity, critical thinking, and a love of learning in my students?

How do I respond when a student is struggling to learn, and what does that reveal about my commitment to their growth?

How am I modeling perseverance, openness to feedback, and lifelong learning in my own professional practice?

In what ways do I foster not only academic achievement but also emotional intelligence and personal development in my students?

Action Step

This week, select one lesson or activity and intentionally redesign it with the explicit goal of "causing to learn"—not just teaching content, but ensuring understanding and engagement for every student.

Chapter 11 - Integrating the Holistic Approach into Everyday Practice

Introduction: The Essence of the Holistic Approach

In the rapidly evolving educational landscape, adopting a holistic approach within everyday classroom practices has become increasingly essential. This model emphasizes the comprehensive development of students, addressing their emotional, social, cognitive, and physical needs. By focusing on the student as an integrated whole, educators can design a learning environment that actively supports and encourages growth across all aspects of student development—intellectual, personal, social, and emotional.

A holistic approach underscores the importance of creating learning experiences that resonate personally with students, ensuring educational relevance and deepening engagement. Educators employing this methodology tailor their instruction to acknowledge diverse learning styles, interests, and personal contexts, thus promoting a deeper connection to the curriculum and fostering intrinsic motivation. Practical strategies to implement such an approach include collaborative projects, mindfulness activities, emotional intelligence training, and culturally responsive teaching practices. These methods empower students by cultivating critical thinking, emotional resilience, and social competence alongside traditional academic skills.

This chapter provides actionable guidance for integrating holistic strategies into classroom instruction, highlights exemplary teachers who successfully embody and model this inclusive pedagogy, and candidly explores common challenges educators face. It further proposes solutions to effectively blend servant leadership principles—prioritizing empathy, listening, and community engagement—with accountability frameworks that ensure measurable educational outcomes. By harmonizing these concepts, educators can create balanced, nurturing classrooms that equip students not only with academic proficiency but also with essential life skills, preparing them comprehensively for future success.

Practical Tips for Implementing a Holistic Approach

Seamlessly integrating a holistic approach requires thoughtful adaptation of teaching methodologies and classroom management.

Create an Inclusive Learning Environment: Creating an inclusive learning environment is fundamental for fostering student success, engagement, and emotional well-being. To build such an environment, educators should actively encourage open communication, mutual respect, and empathy among students. One effective way to achieve this is by designing and implementing collaborative activities that require students to interact in diverse and varied groups. This not only facilitates deeper understanding among peers from different backgrounds and perspectives but also allows students to appreciate and value the unique contributions that everyone brings to the learning community.

Educators should deliberately structure these collaborative experiences to ensure equitable participation, encouraging all students to share ideas and voice their opinions in a safe and supportive setting. Utilizing structured group tasks, such as cooperative learning projects, peer mentoring, role-playing scenarios, or discussion-based assignments, educators can promote inclusive dynamics and interpersonal skill development.

Moreover, incorporating reflective discussions after group activities can help students become more aware of their own assumptions and biases, fostering deeper empathy and mutual understanding. Classroom agreements or community norms can be collectively established, empowering students to hold themselves and each other accountable for maintaining a respectful and welcoming learning space.

By thoughtfully facilitating these inclusive practices, educators create classrooms where students feel valued, respected, and motivated to learn collaboratively and respectfully.

Integrating Social-Emotional Learning (SEL) into the curriculum is essential for nurturing students' emotional intelligence and overall well-being. SEL equips students with valuable skills including empathy, self-regulation, conflict resolution, and effective interpersonal communication. (Mesibov & Drmacich, 2022) By embedding these skills into daily educational practices, educators empower students to successfully navigate personal challenges, build positive relationships, and foster a harmonious classroom environment.

One effective strategy for integrating SEL is to implement structured morning circles or daily check-in sessions. During these gatherings, students have the opportunity to express their feelings, share personal experiences, and discuss challenges in a supportive and structured setting. Such forums provide valuable platforms for students to actively listen to peers, practice empathy, and offer constructive feedback. These sessions also enable educators to monitor students' emotional states, identify areas needing support, and proactively address emerging conflicts or emotional needs.

Beyond daily circles, educators can seamlessly incorporate SEL competencies throughout academic subjects by linking emotional literacy and self-reflection to content areas. For example, literature lessons can highlight character emotions and conflicts, prompting reflective discussions about empathy and emotional responses. Science or social studies topics can be explored through perspectives that emphasize understanding diverse viewpoints, managing disagreements constructively, and appreciating collaborative problem-solving.

Additionally, intentional teaching of self-regulation techniques such as deep breathing exercises, mindfulness, and calming strategies can be embedded within transitions and challenging academic tasks. Incorporating regular SEL-focused activities across curricula not only bolsters academic outcomes but also significantly enhances classroom climate, student resilience, and overall emotional health.

Promote Experiential Learning: Promoting experiential learning within educational settings significantly enhances student engagement, comprehension, and retention. Project-based learning provides an ideal vehicle for students to actively connect classroom theory with practical applications in their daily lives and broader communities. By participating in projects that address real-world challenges, students gain invaluable insights, develop critical thinking abilities, and strengthen their problem-solving skills.

For instance, experiential learning projects can involve students in organizing community service initiatives. Students might research local social issues, collaboratively design and implement actionable solutions, and later reflect on their experiences through structured discussions and journaling activities. Such projects enable students to see firsthand the positive impact they can have on their surroundings, enhancing their sense of social responsibility and community engagement. Additionally, simulations or role-playing scenarios in areas such as economics, government, or history allow students to experience and better understand complex concepts and systems. Students may engage in mock elections, simulated marketplaces, or historical re-enactments, providing hands-on involvement that makes abstract concepts tangible and memorable.

In a math class, students can engage in experiential learning by creating and managing a class business or store. Through this project, students apply mathematical skills such as budgeting, pricing, calculating profit margins, and handling transactions. This practical application allows students to directly experience how mathematical concepts function in real-world settings, enhancing their understanding and appreciation for mathematics.

Through these varied forms of experiential learning, educators can facilitate meaningful and immersive experiences. Students become active participants in their own education, developing not only academic skills but also fostering personal growth, empathy, civic awareness, and lifelong learning habits.

Differentiate Instruction: Differentiated instruction involves recognizing and addressing the diverse learning styles, interests, and abilities of students within a classroom. To effectively implement this teaching strategy, educators should tailor their instructional methods, materials, and assessments to provide multiple pathways for students to engage with and demonstrate their understanding of content.

One practical example of differentiating instruction is through flexible grouping. Rather than using static groups, teachers can organize students into various groups based on skill level, interests, or learning preferences. For instance, during a math lesson on fractions, a teacher might form three distinct groups: one focused on foundational fraction concepts using manipulatives like fraction bars, another tackling more complex fraction problems through collaborative group work, and a third group exploring advanced fraction concepts independently or with enrichment challenges.

Another specific strategy involves offering students choices in how they demonstrate their knowledge. In a literature class, after studying a novel, students could select from several assessment options, such as writing a traditional analytical essay, creating a visual storyboard summarizing key events, or presenting a character analysis through an oral presentation or dramatic monologue. This method ensures each student can leverage their strengths and express their learning effectively.

Teachers can also differentiate content by adjusting the complexity of reading materials and resources provided to students. For example, during a science unit on ecosystems, advanced learners might be given research articles or scientific journals to explore intricate ecological relationships, while struggling readers receive visually engaging infographics, simplified texts, or videos covering fundamental ecosystem concepts.

Moreover, differentiated instruction can include incorporating technology to meet diverse learning needs. Utilizing digital tools like educational apps, online simulations, and interactive websites allows students who thrive through visual or interactive experiences to engage deeply with the content. For example, when studying historical events, students might choose to explore interactive timelines, participate in virtual field trips, or analyze multimedia documentaries.

Finally, incorporating various instructional methods within the same lesson can support differentiation effectively. Teachers might begin a lesson with direct instruction, move into guided collaborative activities, and then allow for independent or small-group exploration, thus catering to auditory, visual, and kinesthetic learners simultaneously. By clearly implementing these differentiated instructional strategies, educators create inclusive learning environments where all students have equitable opportunities to succeed, actively engaging learners based on their individual strengths, interests, and needs.

Exemplary Teachers and Their Holistic Classrooms
Some educators have become paragons of the holistic approach, creating classrooms that reflect this model's principles.

The Responsive Teacher: Consider Ms. Lila, a fifth-grade teacher who begins each day with a community circle. This practice sets a positive tone and allows students to express their thoughts and emotions. Ms. Lila integrates arts into her lessons to cater to diverse intelligences and provides numerous project-based learning opportunities that connect academic concepts to students' lives.

The Innovative Curriculum Leader: Mr. Johnston transformed his high school history class by using experiential learning strategies. He designed a unit where students conducted oral history interviews with the local community, capturing personal narratives that brought historical events to life. This approach engaged students emotionally and cognitively while connecting the curriculum to real-world experience.

The Nurturing Guide: Ms. Kimberly employs mindfulness techniques in her elementary classroom, helping students practice deep breathing and yoga before starting lessons. This routine enhances students' self-awareness and focus, creating a supportive learning environment where students feel centered and ready to engage.

Challenges and Solutions in Implementing Servant Leadership and Accountability
While beneficial, the integration of holistic approaches, including aspects like servant leadership, accountability, and limited resources, can present challenges.

Balancing Servant Leadership with Authority: Balancing servant leadership with authority in the classroom can present a genuine challenge for educators, as they strive to uphold discipline and structure while embodying empathetic, supportive, and stewardship-oriented behaviors. Teachers may find themselves caught between maintaining firm expectations and demonstrating compassionate understanding, potentially leading to confusion or uncertainty among students.

To effectively manage this balance, it is crucial for teachers to establish clear, consistent boundaries and guidelines from the outset. Clearly articulating classroom expectations, consequences for specific behaviors, and a shared understanding of classroom routines provides students with a stable, predictable framework. This clarity helps students understand the roles and responsibilities within the classroom environment, allowing them to feel secure and aware of the behavioral expectations.

Equally important is fostering an atmosphere of approachability, empathy, and mutual respect. Teachers can practice servant leadership by genuinely listening to students, showing authentic care for their individual experiences, and demonstrating willingness to support their academic and personal growth. Simple practices such as daily check-ins, open-door policies for student concerns, and regular one-on-one conferences can enhance students' perception of their teacher as both supportive and approachable.

Additionally, educators can model servant leadership through their interactions, demonstrating respectful communication, proactive problem-solving, and consistent empathy. By exemplifying these traits, teachers create a culture of mutual respect, encouraging students to adopt similar attitudes toward their peers and educators. Ultimately, the successful integration of servant leadership with authoritative structure relies on clear communication, consistent boundaries, and authentic empathy, cultivating a harmonious classroom environment where discipline and compassion coexist effectively.

Ensuring Accountability: Ensuring accountability within a holistic educational framework can indeed pose challenges, particularly when educators prioritize emotional well-being and individual student needs alongside academic standards. Balancing sensitivity to emotional development with rigorous accountability standards requires thoughtful, structured approaches that validate both personal growth and educational outcomes.

A practical solution begins with clearly establishing consistent expectations for behavior, effort, participation, and academic performance. By explicitly communicating these expectations from the outset, educators provide students with a transparent understanding of their responsibilities and the standards they are expected to meet. Clarity in these areas ensures that students feel secure and informed, minimizing anxiety or confusion about accountability measures.

Incorporating structured feedback sessions can strengthen accountability by offering students direct, personalized information about their academic and social-emotional progress. Scheduled conferences, both individually and in small groups, allow educators to clearly communicate successes and areas needing improvement. These sessions can help students clearly identify actions required to achieve their goals, further reinforcing accountability.

Another effective strategy is the use of goal-setting frameworks, where students establish achievable short-term and long-term objectives related to their learning and emotional development. Educators can periodically meet with students to review and adjust these goals as needed, emphasizing measurable outcomes such as task completion, skill mastery, and interpersonal improvements. Regular assessments, including quizzes, performance tasks, and collaborative projects, can provide concrete metrics for evaluating student progress.

In addition, fostering peer accountability through collaborative group projects encourages students to support and hold each other responsible. Establishing clear roles and responsibilities within groups helps students recognize their contributions to collective success. Recognizing and celebrating both individual and group accomplishments reinforces the value of accountability, encouraging students to consistently strive for improvement within a supportive and clearly structured learning environment.

Resource and Training Limitations: Resource and Training Limitations present significant barriers to effectively adopting holistic educational strategies. Educators frequently encounter challenges such as inadequate materials, limited access to specialized training, or insufficient institutional support to fully implement these beneficial practices within their classrooms. To overcome these obstacles, educators can actively leverage peer collaboration as a valuable resource. Establishing collaborative teacher networks within schools or districts can enable educators to share effective strategies, materials, and insights into holistic teaching practices. Regularly scheduled collaborative sessions or peer mentorship programs offer platforms for educators to learn from each other's experiences, enhancing collective professional growth.

Additionally, a wealth of readily available online resources can serve as practical solutions to resource constraints. Free online workshops, webinars, instructional videos, and comprehensive lesson plans dedicated to holistic education provide accessible and cost-effective means for educators to enhance their instructional repertoire. Digital communities and forums also allow teachers to exchange ideas, troubleshoot issues, and continuously update their holistic teaching methodologies.

Schools and districts should prioritize targeted professional development focused explicitly on holistic education to equip teachers comprehensively. By systematically investing in workshops, seminars, or training programs that address emotional intelligence, differentiated instruction, social-emotional learning, and mindfulness practices, educational institutions can effectively bridge existing training gaps. Such institutional support demonstrates a commitment to holistic education, empowering educators with the necessary tools, confidence, and competence to implement these strategies successfully, ultimately benefiting student development and achievement.

Conclusion: Towards a Collaborative Educational Future

Integrating the holistic approach into everyday classroom practices signifies a transformative shift toward nurturing well-rounded individuals equipped with not only intellectual acumen but also emotional intelligence and social skills. The teachers highlighted in this chapter represent the catalysts of change, demonstrating that, despite the challenges, it is possible to create educational spaces that are inclusive, experiential, and emotionally supportive.

The journey toward holistic education requires thoughtful effort, creativity, and commitment to unlocking each student's potential fully. Through a balance of servant leadership, accountability, and personalized learning, educators can pave the way for an educational paradigm that prepares students to flourish in all aspects of life. With continued advocacy for resource allocation, professional development, and adaptable assessment methods, such an approach can foster both individual and collective growth, contributing to better, more compassionate learning communities.

The dynamic field of education constantly seeks to equip future generations with the skills and knowledge needed to thrive in an ever-changing world. In this quest, the holistic approach stands out as a transformative model capable of redefining educational practices for teachers and students alike. This approach heralds a shift from traditional education, emphasizing not only intellectual development but also fostering emotional and social growth. By reinforcing the transformative potential of the holistic approach, this conclusion aims to inspire educators to embrace these principles and provide a glimpse of the comprehensive roadmap discussed in this book.

Reflection and Action Step

How do I currently demonstrate empathy and active listening in my classroom, and how can I further strengthen these servant leadership qualities to better support my students?

In what ways do I foster a classroom environment that prioritizes healing, awareness, and stewardship for all students—especially those facing personal or academic challenges?

How do I intentionally recognize and celebrate the growth and achievements of each student, not just their final outcomes?

What new relationship-building strategy can I try with my current students to better connect with those who seem less engaged or more reserved?

How can I use my own values—such as respect, compassion, and responsibility—to set a positive example in my classroom?

Action Step

Identify one student who appears disengaged or reserved and commit to a specific, intentional relationship-building action this week.

Chapter 12 - The Transformative Potential of the Holistic Approach

At its core, the holistic approach to education is about nurturing the whole child. This model underscores the interconnectedness of cognitive, emotional, and social dimensions, recognizing that true learning extends beyond mere academic excellence. For teachers, adopting a holistic approach transforms not only their pedagogical methods but also their relationships with students and their roles as educators. Teachers incorporating holistic principles become facilitators of a learning environment that acknowledges the diverse needs and potentials of each student. They move beyond simply conveying information to actively fostering a setting where students are empowered and encouraged to explore, question, and connect with the world in meaningful ways.

For students, the holistic approach offers the opportunity to develop a comprehensive skill set essential for success in various life domains. This model advocates for an education system where students learn to engage critically with content, appreciate the value of empathy and collaboration, and cultivate resilience. Transformative educational experiences ignite a lifelong love for learning, equipping students with adaptable capabilities that extend well beyond classroom walls.

A Call to Action for Educators

Educators hold a pivotal role in spearheading the adoption of holistic methods. By embracing this approach, teachers are encouraged to reevaluate and evolve their teaching strategies, prioritizing students' comprehensive growth. Here are key actions educators can undertake to integrate holistic principles effectively:

Expand Teaching Methodologies: Educators are urged to diversify their instructional approaches, incorporating experiential, project-based, and inquiry-led learning methods. These strategies cultivate a deeper connection between students and their learning materials, facilitating critical thinking and real-world application.

Cultivate Emotional Intelligence: Fostering emotional intelligence is a cornerstone of the holistic approach. Teachers should prioritize social-emotional learning in their classrooms, integrating activities that encourage students to understand and regulate their emotions and develop empathy and strong interpersonal skills.

Foster Community and Collaboration: Building a classroom culture that emphasizes community and collaboration is essential. Teachers should encourage peer-to-peer interactions and group projects that harness the collective strengths of students, nurturing a sense of belonging and shared responsibility.

Engage in Continuous Professional Development: To effectively adopt holistic practices, ongoing professional development is crucial. Educators are urged to seek out training opportunities, engage in reflective practices, and collaborate with peers to refine their skills.

Advocate for Institutional Support: Teachers should advocate for systemic changes that support holistic practices, including curriculum adaptations, allocation of resources, and collaboration with families and communities. Creating a school-wide culture that embraces holistic education requires collective commitment and structural adjustments.

Conclusion: Towards a Formidable Force of the Holistic Approach

In conclusion, the holistic approach stands as a formidable force in reshaping the educational experience for teachers and students. By embracing this methodology, educators commit to fostering environments that celebrate the rich tapestry of student growth, characterized by intellectual curiosity, emotional intelligence, and social awareness. Through this chapter, an actionable framework was presented, providing the insights, encouragement, and tools to revolutionize classrooms and forge a meaningful path ahead.

As advocates and pioneers of change, educators are called upon to champion this transformation, nurturing generations of thinkers, collaborators, and empathetic leaders. The holistic approach is more than an educational philosophy—it is a movement inspiring a more inclusive, interconnected world, where learning and life skills thrive ever in harmony. It is with sincere hope that this discourse propels educators on a collective journey toward an enriched, dynamic, and human-centric educational future.

Reflection and Action Step

How do I intentionally motivate students who may be discouraged or lack confidence, especially in challenging subject areas?

In what ways do I make learning relevant and engaging for students who are not naturally interested in the material?

What steps do I take to help students set and achieve realistic, personalized learning goals?

How do I recognize and celebrate student effort and progress, not just final outcomes?

What strategies can I use to help students overcome negative beliefs about their abilities, such as "I'm just not a math person"?

Action Step

At the start of a new unit, have each student set a personal learning goal related to the subject (e.g., mastering a specific concept or improving a test score). Frame the learning process as a journey toward achieving something meaningful to them. Regularly remind students that, like athletes coached to push beyond their comfort zones, they are working toward their own aspirations—even when the work feels challenging. Use encouraging, coaching-style language to reinforce that overcoming difficulties is part of reaching their goals.

Bibliography

Bandura, A. (1997). *Sef:Efficacy: The Exercise of Control*. WH Freeman.

Boaler, J. (2015). *Mathematical Mindsets : Unleashing Students' Potential Through Creative Math, Inspiring Messages and Innovative Teaching,*. San Francisco: John Wiley & Sons, Incorporated .

Dweck, C. S. (2007). *The New Psychology of Success*. New York: Ballantine Books.

Glimcher, P. W. (2011, March 9). *Understanding dopamine and reinforcement learning: The dopamine reward prediction error hypothesis*. Retrieved May 4, 2025, from https://www.pnas.org/doi/10.1073/pnas.1014269108

Greenleaf, R. K. (1964). *The Servant as Leader*. South Orange, NJ: The Greenleaf Center for Servant Leadership.

Gueldner, B. A., Feuerborn, L. L., & Merrell, K. W. (2010). *Social and Emotional Learning in the Classroom (Second Edition)*. New York: Guilford Press.

Hess, H. (1956). *The Journey to the East*. New York: Picador.

Kuhnert, D. (2016). *Servant Leadership: Influencing Others to Get There. by Leading a Transformational Life*. Author House.

Mazur, E. (1997). *Peer Instruction: A User's Manual*. Upper Saddle River: Prentice Hall.

Mendler, A. (2011). *Motivating Students Who Don't Care: Successful Techniques for Educators*. New York: Solution Tree.

Mesibov, D., & Drmacich, D. (2022). *Helping Students Take Control of Their Own Learning: 279 Learner-Centered, Social-Emotional Strategies for Teachers*. New York: Routledge.

Pianta, R. C., Hamre, B. K., & Allen, J. P. (2012). Teacher-Student Relationships and Engagement: Conceptualizing, Measuring, and Improving the Capacity of Classroom Interaction. In S. Christianson, A. Reschly, & C. Whylie, *Handbook of Research on Student Engagement* (pp. 365-386). New York: Springer.

Ryan, R. M., & Deci, E. L. (2017). *Self-Determination Theory: Basic Psychological Needs in Motivation, Development, and Wellness*. New York: The Gilford Press.

Shirley, D., & Hargreaves, A. (1995). *Five Paths of Student Engagement*. Bloomington: Solution Tree Press.
Whitney, D. S. (2014). *Spiritual Disciplines for the Christian Life*. Carol Stream: Tyndale House Publishers, Inc.